D0873672

ESTATES, FUTURE INTERESTS, *AND* POWERS OF APPOINTMENT

IN A NUTSHELL

FIFTH EDITION

By

THOMAS P. GALLANIS
N. William Hines Chair in Law
University of Iowa

LAWRENCE W. WAGGONER
Lewis M. Simes Professor Emeritus of Law
University of Michigan

WEST
ACADEMIC
PUBLISHING

Mat #41556123

Nutshell Series, In a Nutshell and the Nutshell Logo are trademarks registered in the U.S. Patent and Trademark Office.

COPYRIGHT © 1981, 1993 By LAWRENCE W. WAGGONER
© West, a Thomson business 2005
© 2010 Thomson Reuters
© 2014 LEG, Inc. d/b/a West Academic

  610 Opperman Drive

  St. Paul, MN 55123

  1-800-313-9378

West, West Academic Publishing, and West Academic are trademarks of West Publishing Corporation, used under license.

Printed in the United States of America

ISBN: 978-0-314-29096-0

ESTATES, FUTURE INTERESTS, *AND* POWERS OF APPOINTMENT

IN A NUTSHELL

PREFACE

The objective of this book is to help law students understand the law of estates, future interests, and powers of appointment. First-year students in Property and upper-year students in Wills and Trusts are the intended audience.

It is fitting that the Nutshell Series includes *Estates, Future Interests, and Powers of Appointment* in its inventory of titles. It was in the future interests area that putting a body of law into a nutshell appears to have emerged. The case was *Van Grutten v. Foxwell*, [1897] App. Cas. 658 (H.L.). In the course of his opinion, Lord

Macnaghten referred to Lord Thurlow's statement about the Rule in Shelley's Case as one that put "the case in a nutshell."* Lord Macnaghten added, however, that it is "one thing to put a case like *Shelley's* into a nutshell and another thing to keep it there." The warning is apt. Oversimplifying the law can be as unwise as discussing every mind-numbing nuance.

Our aim is to navigate between the two extremes. This book puts the law of estates, future interests, and powers of appointment into a nutshell, clarifying and explaining the law without oversimplification.

In 2010, the American Law Institute approved the final chapters of the Restatement Third of Property: Wills and Other Donative Transfers (cited herein as the Restatement 3d of Property). These chapters contain a new approach to the classification of present and future interests and a reformulation of

---

*Lord Thurlow, it should be noted for the sake of accuracy, never himself undertook to put the Rule in Shelley's Case into a nutshell. His statement about the rule was contained in a letter he wrote to Francis Hargrave. The letter is published in 3 Francis Hargrave, Jurisconsult Exercitations 360 (1813).

and a reformulation of the Rule Against Perpetuities. One of us (Lawrence W. Waggoner) was the Reporter for this Restatement. We discuss the Restatement's innovations in this *Nutshell*. See also the following articles:

Lawrence W. Waggoner, The American Law Institute Proposes Simplifying the Doctrine of Estates, University of Michigan Public Law Working Paper No. 198 (2010), available at http://ssrn.com/abstract=1612878.

Lawrence. W. Waggoner, The Case for Curtailing Dead-Hand Control: The American Law Institute Declares the Perpetual-Trust Movement Ill Advised, University of Michigan Public Law Working Paper No. 199 (2010), available at http://ssrn.com/abstract =1614934.

Lawrence W. Waggoner, The American Law Institute Proposes a New Approach to Perpetuities: Limiting the Dead Hand to Two Younger Generations, University of Michigan Public Law Working Paper No. 200 (2010), available at http://ssrn.com/abstract=1614936.

PREFACE

This edition also incorporates the Uniform Powers of Appointment Act, approved by the Uniform Law Commission in 2013. Professor Gallanis was the Reporter for the Act.

We wish to thank Foundation Press for granting us permission to adapt portions of Thomas P. Gallanis, *Family Property Law: Cases and Materials on Wills, Trusts, and Future Interests* (5th ed. 2011) (formerly co-authored with Lawrence W. Waggoner, Gregory S. Alexander, and Mary Louise Fellows), for use in the material herein.

For the production of this Fifth Edition, research support from the University of Iowa Law School is gratefully acknowledged.

THOMAS P. GALLANIS
LAWRENCE W. WAGGONER

Iowa City, Iowa
Ann Arbor, Michigan

September 2013

OUTLINE

Page

PART I. POSSESSORY ESTATES AND FUTURE INTERESTS

OUTLINE

Page

Page

OUTLINE

Page

PART II. MARITAL ESTATES

OUTLINE

Page

OUTLINE

TABLE OF ABBREVIATIONS

———

ALI	American Law Institute
Am. L. Prop.	American Law of Property (A. James Casner ed. 1952)
Bl. Com.	William Blackstone, Commentaries on the Law of England (1st ed. 1765-1769)
Gray on Perpetuities	John Chipman Gray, The Rule Against Perpetuities (4th ed. 1942)
IRC	Internal Revenue Code (1986 and subsequent amendments)
MMPA	Model Marital Property Act (1983 and subsequent amendments)

TABLE OF ABBREVIATIONS

NCCUSL	National Conference of Commissioners on Uniform State Laws
Restatement of Property	Restatement of Property (1936, 1940, 1944)
Restatement 2d of Property	Restatement (Second) of Property (Donative Transfers) (1983, 1986, 1988, 1992)
Restatement 3d of Property	Restatement (Third) of Property (Wills and Other Donative Transfers) (1999, 2003, 2011)
Restatement 2d of Trusts	Restatement (Second) of Trusts (1959)

TABLE OF ABBREVIATIONS

Restatement 3d of Trusts	Restatement (Third) of Trusts (2003, 2007, and 2012)
Simes & Smith on Future Interests	Lewis M. Simes & Allan F. Smith, The Law of Future Interests (2d ed. 1956, John A. Borron 3d ed. 2002)
Thompson on Real Property	Thompson on Real Property (David A. Thomas ed. 1994–)
Uniform Rule	Uniform Statutory Rule Against Perpetuities (1986, amended 1990)
UPC	Uniform Probate Code (1990 and subsequent amendments)
UTC	Uniform Trust Code (2000 and subsequent amendments)

TABLE OF CASES

References are to Pages

———

TABLE OF CASES

TABLE OF CASES

TABLE OF CASES

TABLE OF CASES

ESTATES,
FUTURE INTERESTS,
AND
POWERS OF
APPOINTMENT

IN A NUTSHELL

Fifth Edition

CHAPTER 1

INTRODUCTION TO ESTATES AND FUTURE INTERESTS

§ 1.1 Fragmentation of Ownership

Our legal system, like many others in the world, permits outright ownership of property. When speaking of personal property, we refer to *outright ownership* or *absolute ownership*. When speaking of land, we use the phrase ownership in *fee simple absolute*. Whatever the type of property, outright ownership carries with it several rights, known as incidents of ownership. Two important incidents of ownership are the right to possess the property (meaning the right to use it and exclude others from using it) and to transfer ownership to another (inter vivos or at death).

1

Our legal system also permits ownership to be divided or fragmented. Derived from the English common law, fragmentation of ownership is an ingenious concept. To understand what the concept means, it is important to understand what it does *not* mean: the concept does not **mean** dividing property into tangible segments, each owned by a different person. (That type of division is readily possible under our legal system, but it is hardly an ingenious concept.) The ingenuity of fragmentation is that it allows two or more persons to have simultaneous interests in the property as a whole. Fragmentation of ownership involves an allocation of the incidents of ownership among the owners. The manner of allocation depends to a great extent on the form of fragmentation.

There are three basic forms of fragmentation. First, ownership can be fragmented into *concurrent* interests; these are the familiar tenancy in common, joint tenancy, and tenancy by the entirety (see Chapter 9). Secondly, ownership can be fragmented into *legal* and *equitable* interests; this arises when property is placed in trust. Finally, ownership can be fragmented sequentially into *present* and *future* interests; a future interest in property is a nonpossessory interest that might or will become possessory at some future time.

For an easy example of fragmentation, think of an apartment rented by a landlord to a tenant. The tenant has some rights to the apartment; the landlord has other rights. Who owns the apartment? The answer is that the incidents of ownership have been divided or fragmented between the tenant and the landlord. A metaphor often used to capture this idea of fragmentation is the metaphor of property rights as a *bundle of sticks*. In our example, some sticks are held by the tenant, others by the landlord.

A second example will drive home the point. Many first-year Property casebooks contain the case of *Gruen v. Gruen*, 68 N.Y.2d 48, 496 N.E.2d 869 (1986). That case concerned a father's gift of a painting to his son. The father did not give the painting outright. Instead, the father gave the son the right to possess the painting after the father's death; until then, the father retained the right of possession. The question facing the court was whether the father had made a gift during his lifetime or whether the gift occurred only at the father's death. (If the transfer occurred at the father's death, the gift would have had to have been made in accordance with the formalities of a validly executed will.) The court held that the father had fragmented ownership of the painting during his lifetime. Some sticks in the bundle had been retained by the father while others had been transferred to the son.

Gruen illustrates the important distinction between *present interests* (also known as *possessory* or *present estates*[1]) and *future interests*. It is crucial to understand these terms. A common misunderstanding is to think that the words "present" and "future" distinguish between interests that are currently created and interests that are created in the future. This is not the distinction. *Both present and future interests are already created.* That is why the court in *Gruen* correctly held that the father had made a current gift to the

---

[1] The term *possessory estate* or *present estate* is more apt when referring to an interest in land, whereas the term *present interest* is more apt when referring to the income interest of a trust beneficiary, for that beneficiary has a present right to the income generated by the trust property, but not a present right to possession of the trust property.

The Restatement of Property defines the word *estate* to mean an interest in land that is or might become possessory and is ownership measured in terms of duration. The Restatement defines the word *interest* to mean either (1) varying aggregates of rights, privileges, powers, and immunities or (2) any one of them. See Restatement of Property §§ 5, 9.

son: he had made a current gift of a future interest while retaining for himself a present interest.

A present interest is a right to current possession; a future interest is an interest in which possession is postponed (and depending on the terms of the future interest, possession might or might not occur eventually).

In *Gruen*, both the father and the son held interests in property. The interests were transferable and could be attached by creditors. The only distinction is that the father's interest was currently possessory, while the son's was currently nonpossessory. Put differently: the use of the word "future" in the term "future interest" refers not to when the interest is created but when (if ever) the right to possession arises. The son did not receive his interest in the future but rather at the very moment when the father fragmented the ownership of the painting.

§ 1.2   A Limit on Fragmentation: The *Numerus Clausus* Principle

The ability of property owners to fragment their interests raises an obvious question: can the fragmentation take only previously-defined forms or can owners subdivide the interests in any manner they wish? The answer is that owners can use only the fixed number of previously-defined forms of property fragmentation. This is known as the principle of the *numerus clausus* (Latin for "closed number").

The principle is well illustrated by a case included in some first-year Property books, *Johnson v. Whiton*, 309 Mass. 571, 34 N.E. 542 (1893). That case concerned the interpretation of a will. The will devised property to the testator's granddaughter Sarah "and her heirs on her father's side." As we shall see in Chapter 2, this language does not correspond to any of the recognized estates. One possibility for the court would have been to say that the testator fragmented the property in a new way. But instead, the court emphasized that "a man cannot create a new kind of inheritance" and construed the disposition to come within an accepted form (the fee simple absolute, on which see § 2.3). Put differently: the categories of estates and future interests are fixed; the law does not empower a transferor to create a new form of fragmentation. What a man cannot do, however, can be done by the government. The *numerus clausus* principle does not prevent a legislature from creating a new kind of estate. The legislatures of some states have done this, for example by combining community property with a right of survivorship. See, e.g., Ariz. Rev. Stat. § 33-431; Cal. Civ. Code § 682.1. (On community property with right of survivorship, see § 8.5 note 8.)

The *numerus clausus* principle is well established in precedent, but what is its rationale? The scholarly literature on this point is not abundant. For an often-cited analysis, see Thomas W. Merrill & Henry E. Smith, Optimal Standardization in the Law of Property: The *Numerus Clausus* Principle, 110 Yale L.J. 1 (2000). But are Merrill & Smith persuasive? Should rights in property be more standardized than rights in contract? See Joshua A.T. Fairfield, The Cost of Consent: Optimal Standardization in the Law of Contract, 58 Emory L.J. 1401 (2009).

The effect of the *numerus clausus* principle is to limit the forms of fragmentation. This has a beneficial by-product in the classroom: students need only learn a fixed number of estates and future interests, and how to recognize them.

§ 1.3   Coverage of This Book

The fragmentation of property in American law takes three main forms, corresponding to the first three parts of this book. Part I examines the temporal division of property into present and future interests. Part II examines the rights given by law to one spouse in the other spouse's property (known traditionally as the "marital estates"). Part III examines the concurrent division of property among multiple present owners ("concurrent estates").

In addition to covering these three topics, the book examines in Part IV an important device for delegating control over interests in property: the power of appointment.

Of the four topics, the most complex is the first: the law of present estates and future interests. It is appropriate to say a word about why this topic is so important.

§ 1.4   The Importance of Future Interests

The law of future interests developed in the context of interests created directly in land, known as *legal* interests because they were enforceable in the English courts of common law. Such interests are not commonly created today. Instead, future interests appear mainly in trusts.

Trusts, which often hold securities (a form of personal property) and may or may not hold land, combine two types of fragmentation of ownership. First, "legal" title to the trust property is held by the trustee and "equitable" title is held by the trust beneficiaries. These labels in quotation marks derive from England, where for many centuries the courts of common law recognized the ownership of the trustee, while the Court of Chancery, administering equity, enforced the rights of the beneficiaries. The fusion of law and equity occurred in England in the nineteenth century, yet it is still conceptually accurate and helpful to think of a fragmentation of title between the trustee and the beneficiaries. Second, most trusts have multiple beneficiaries, with the equitable title divided among them in terms of time, i.e., between income beneficiaries and corpus beneficiaries. Think, for example, of a family with husband, wife, and two children. Who knows which spouse will die first? The husband and wife might each provide by will that a trust should be established for the lifetime of the surviving spouse, with the balance of the property to go at the surviving spouse's death to the then-living children. In this example, the equitable or beneficial interest in the trust is divided temporally between the surviving spouse and the children.

Trusts are mainstays of modern law practice. There are no reliable statistics about the total number of trusts in existence or about their aggregate value, because many trusts are privately created and managed. However, the federal government compiles statistics about trusts in which the trustee is a federally insured commercial or savings bank. In 2011, the most recent year for which such data are available, there were approximately 780,000 such trusts having an aggregate market value of approximately $860 billion.

With such wealth held in trust, most lawyers and law students should know something about future interests. Hence Part I of this book.

§ 1.5   A   Word   About   the Hypothetical Examples Used in This Book

Hypothetical examples are used throughout this book to supplement and illustrate the text.

The hypothetical examples usually involve legal interests directly in land. This has been done to simplify the wording. As pointed out earlier (recall § 1.4), such interests are not commonly created today. Present and future interests are more commonly created in trusts. Nevertheless, the process of classification is easier to understand if illustrated by examples that say "*G* transferred land to *A* for life, remainder to *B*," rather than the wordier "*G* transferred securities to the Faithful Bank, in trust, to pay the income to *A* for life, and at *A*'s death to deliver the trust assets to *B*."

Whether the transfer was a conveyance (inter vivos transfer) or a devise (testamentary transfer) makes no difference in most of the examples. The generic word "transfer" is used in those cases. If the type of transfer makes a difference, the term "conveyance" or "devise" is used, as appropriate.

Unless otherwise stated, you should assume that the grantor, *G*, owned the property outright (i.e., in fee simple absolute) when *G* made the transfer.

The examples serve two functions. They aid initial understanding by illustrating the principles stated abstractly in the text. They also aid exam preparation by serving as review questions. Each example is arranged so that the facts and solution are given in separate paragraphs. This allows you to test your ability to answer each problem by covering up the solution, and then to check your answer.

It may help you to understand the examples if you make a linear chart of the facts as they develop over time. Starting with horizontal lines depicting the lifetimes of the transferor and transferees, insert in the horizontal lines the following symbols: $\otimes$ to indicate a person's death; $\downarrow$ to indicate the time and direction of a transfer; and $+$ to indicate the time when an interest or estate of a living person changes into another interest or estate. To illustrate this technique, take a devise of land by G "to A for life, remainder to B." If B survived A, the case can be charted as follows:

$G{\rightarrow}\otimes$
$A{\rightarrow}\downarrow{\leftarrow}$(life estate)$\longrightarrow\otimes$
$B{\rightarrow}\downarrow{\leftarrow}$(remainder)$\rightarrow+{\leftarrow}(fsa)\rightarrow$

Your chart shows that when the life tenant, A, died, B's remainder became a fee simple absolute.

To take a more complex example, suppose that G devised land "to A for life, then to B if B survives A, but if not to C." If B predeceased A but C survived A, the case can be charted as follows:

$G{\rightarrow}\otimes$
$A{\rightarrow}\downarrow{\leftarrow}$(l/e)————————————$\rightarrow\otimes$
$B{\rightarrow}\downarrow{\leftarrow}$(cont rem)$\rightarrow\otimes$
$C{\rightarrow}\downarrow{\leftarrow}$(cont rem)$\rightarrow+{\leftarrow}$(vested rem)$\rightarrow+{\leftarrow}(fsa)\rightarrow$

Your chart shows that when *B* died, *C*'s contingent remainder became a vested remainder (see infra § 3.11), and when *A* died, *C*'s vested remainder became a fee simple absolute.

§ 1.6   Additional Exercises (and Answers)

In addition to the examples in text, the *Nutshell* contains practice questions. The questions cover Part I; Parts II and III together; and Part IV. They are found at pages **XXX**, **XXX**, and **XXX**, respectively. The answers appear in the back of the book, starting at page **XXX**.

PART I

POSSESSORY ESTATES
AND
FUTURE INTERESTS

CHAPTER 2

CLASSIFYING POSSESSORY ESTATES (A.K.A. PRESENT INTERESTS)

§ 2.1   A Word About Classification

Classification means fixing the proper label or labels to a possessory estate or future interest. "Possessory estate" means an ownership interest in property granting the owner the current right to possession or enjoyment. "Future interest" means an ownership interest in property in which the right to possession or enjoyment is deferred until some time in the future; the future possession or enjoyment may or may not be certain to occur.

17

The hierarchy of possessory estates and future interests is a refined, artificial structure that took centuries to develop fully. If it had been designed in one fell swoop, the flexibility it provides estate planners and clients of today could readily be achieved with a system of much greater simplicity. Indeed, the American Law Institute has promulgated a simplified system of possessory estates and future interests in the Restatement 3d of Property. In this *Nutshell*, we cover both the traditional and the simplified systems.

The complexity and artificiality in the traditional system evolved, step by step over a fairly long period of time, from the struggles of competing interest groups. The owners of the great landed estates in England, assisted by ingenious lawyers, sought to avoid the death taxes of the day and to safeguard their estates through the generations. As one loophole was plugged in favor of enforcing the tax or promoting freer alienability and control for the recipients of the property, the ingenious lawyers found another. The result was that great distinctions were drawn on the basis of the words used in creating the dispositions. Through classification, different ways of saying the same thing were accorded different legal consequences. Form controlled over substance. In classification, form still controls over substance. Form controls legal consequences less than before, however, because the legal consequences flowing from classification gradually have been reduced.

As we study the traditional system, bear in mind that the system of classification, which was developed in earlier centuries mainly for legal interests in land, has been transposed today to the classification of the equitable interests in the modern trust. (Recall the discussion in § 1.4.)

§ 2.2   Three Terms of Art: Quantum, Freehold, and Particular Estate

The possessory estates are traditionally ordered in a hierarchy by *quantum*. In descending order of quantum, the groupings are: (1) fee simple estate (all fee simple estates are of the same quantum); (2) fee tail; (3) life estate; (4) term of years; (5) estate from period to period; (6) estate at will; and (7) estate at sufferance.

Feudal law in England also distinguished between *freehold* and *nonfreehold* estates. Only the former signified a lifelong bond between a free man and his feudal lord. J.H. Baker, An Introduction to English Legal History 259 (4th ed. 2002). The freehold estates are (1)-(3) above: the fee simple estates; the fee tail; and the life estate. The nonfreehold estates are (4)-(7) above: the term of years; the estate from period to period; the estate at will; and the estate at sufferance.

The term *particular estate* is a term of art denoting any estate that is less than a fee simple—a fee tail, a life estate, a term of years, and so on.

§ 2.3   The Fee Simple Absolute

The estate in *fee simple absolute* is a present interest that is not subject to termination. It is unlimited in duration. As noted earlier in § 1.1, the personal-property counterpart of the fee simple absolute is called absolute ownership or outright ownership. A fee simple absolute is not subject to any special limitations, conditions subsequent, or executory limitations. A fee simple absolute is never followed by a future interest.

At common law, a conveyance simply "to *A*" gave *A* only an interest for life. To convey a fee simple absolute, the transferor was required to include the additional words "and his heirs," as in the following example.

Example 2.1: G conveyed land "to *A* and his heirs."

A has a fee simple absolute.

The words "and his heirs" are known as *words of limitation, not words of purchase*. Words of limitation are words that act to define the estate being transferred. Words of purchase are words that transfer an interest. In Example 2.1, the words "and his heirs" do not transfer an interest to *A*'s heirs; the only person receiving an interest is *A*. The words do describe the type of interest *A* is receiving: a fee simple absolute.[1] Hence, the words

---

[1] Occasionally the language of a disposition might say "*A* or his heirs." While not recommended, the substitution of the "or" for the orthodox "and" will probably not make any difference. The Restatement of Property § 27 cmts. d & e state that "or his heirs" will generally be treated as words of limitation, not words of purchase, especially when they appear in the transfer of a present interest.

A transfer to "*A* and his children" is ambiguous. *Wild's Case*, 6 Coke Rep. 16b, 77 Eng. Rep. 279 (K.B. 1599), held that if *A* has children at the time of the transfer, *A* and his children take as joint tenants (on which, see § 9.2). The rule in Wild's Case, which applied in England only to devises of land, has been repudiated by the Restatement 3d of Property § 14.2 cmt. f, which construes the transfer as creating a life estate in *A* and a remainder in *A*'s children. For an analogous result in a transfer to "*A* and his issue," see *id.*, § 14.4 cmt. f.

"and his heirs" are words of limitation.

The words "and his heirs" were never required in wills and today are not typically required in inter vivos conveyances. A transfer "to *A*" suffices in most states to give *A* a fee simple absolute.

This *Nutshell* follows modern practice in not using the words "and his heirs" in future interests. The hypotheticals read "to *A* for life, remainder to *B*" rather than "to *A* for life, remainder to *B* and his heirs." The words do appear in hypotheticals creating present interests in fee simple—"to *A* and his heirs so long as..."—even though they are not strictly required.

§ 2.4   Defeasible Fees

The *defeasible fee simple* estates are subject to termination upon the happening of an event specified in the grant.

In the traditional system of classification, there are three defeasible fee simple estates: (1) the fee simple determinable, (2) the fee simple subject to a condition subsequent, and (3) the fee simple subject to an executory limitation. Distinguishing these estates requires an understanding of the concept of "defeasance."

Defeasance means loss of ownership—in other words, that the holder of the possessory estate will lose that estate upon the happening of an event stipulated in the grant. A possessory estate subject to defeasance is either subject to a *limitation* or to a *condition subsequent*.

The distinction between limitations and conditions subsequent is important to learn in order to master the traditional system of classification, but it is difficult for modern students because the distinction is based on the elusive contrast between grants that terminate naturally versus grants that terminate by being cut short.

Possessory estates subject to a "limitation" are said to terminate *naturally* or *by their own terms.* The language in the grant signifying a limitation are words such as "during," "until," "while," "so long as," "for so long as," or simply "for [a designated period]," followed by words such as "at," "upon," or "then." The limitation is called a *special* limitation if it describes an event that is not certain to happen (unlike death, which will happen eventually).

Possessory estates subject to a "condition subsequent" are said to terminate by being *cut short* or *divested* upon the happening of the stipulated event. The language in the grant signifying a condition subsequent are words such as "on condition that" or "provided that," followed by words such as "but if" or "and if." (In some grants, only the "but if" or "and if" language will appear.)

With this background in mind, let us turn to the three kinds of defeasible fee simple estates within the traditional system. They are, again: (1) the fee simple determinable, (2) the fee simple subject to a condition subsequent, and (3) the fee simple subject to an executory limitation.

The *fee simple determinable* is a fee estate subject to a *special limitation,* which means that it automatically terminates if the specified event happens; the specified event is an event not certain to occur.

Example 2.2: G conveyed land "to A and his heirs so long as A does not allow liquor to be sold on the premises; upon A's allowing liquor to be sold on the premises, the property is to revert to me." A's fee simple estate is subject to a limitation that is not certain to occur—a special limitation. Therefore, A has an estate in fee simple determinable.[2]

Example 2.3: G conveyed land "to *A* and his heirs so long as *A* does not allow liquor to be sold on the premises; and upon *A*'s allowing liquor to be sold on the premises, the property is to go to *B*."[3] As in the previous example, *A*'s fee simple estate is subject to a limitation that is not certain to occur—a special limitation. Therefore, *A* has an estate in fee simple determinable.[4]

The *fee simple subject to a condition subsequent* is a fee estate subject to *divestment*—to being cut

[2] The future interest retained by *G* is called a "possibility of reverter" in the traditional system of classification and a "reversion" in the simplified system of classification. See §§ 3.2, 3.3.

[3] The limitation regarding selling liquor applies only to *A* and not to *A*'s successors in interest. Therefore, the executory interest created in *B* is valid under the traditional Rule Against Perpetuities because the interest must vest or fail within *A*'s lifetime.

[4] The future interest created in *B* is called an "executory interest" in the traditional system of classification and a "remainder" in the simplified system of classification. See §§ 3.5, 3.6.

short—in favor of a reversionary[5] future interest called, in the traditional system of classification, a right of entry. The happening of the specified event does not automatically divest the estate; rather, it empowers the grantor (or the grantor's successor in interest) to divest the estate by exercising the right of entry.[6]

Example 2.4: G conveyed land "to *A* and his heirs on condition that *A* not allow liquor to be sold on the premises, and if *A* allows liquor to be sold on the premises, then the grantor is to have the right to re-enter and take possession of the premises." *A* has an estate in fee simple subject to a condition subsequent.[7]

The *fee simple subject to an executory limitation* is a fee estate subject to *divestment*—to being cut short—in favor of a *non*reversionary future interest

---

[5]For the distinction between reversionary and nonreversionary interests, see § 3.1.

[6]The right of entry is known in the simplified system of classification as a "reversion." See § 3.3.

[7]In the traditional system of classification, *G* has a right of entry. In the simplified system of classification, *G* has a reversion. See §§ 3.2, 3.3.

called, in the traditional system of classification, an executory interest.[8] The happening of the specified event divests the estate.

Example 2.5: G conveyed land "to *A* and his heirs, but if *A* allows liquor to be sold on the premises, then to *B*." *A* has an estate in fee simple subject to an executory limitation.[9]

So far, we have described the traditional system. The new Restatement 3d of Property eliminates the distinction among the three fee simple defeasible estates, collapsing the three categories into one category called the *fee simple defeasible*. As defined in the Restatement 3d of Property, the estate in fee simple defeasible "is a present interest that terminates upon the happening of a stated event that might or might not occur." Restatement 3d of Property § 24.3. Thus, in Examples 2.2 through 2.5 above, *A*'s interest under the simplified

---

[8]The executory interest is known in the simplified system of classification as a "remainder." See § 3.6.

[9]In the traditional system of classification, *B* has an executory interest. In the simplified system of classification, *B* has a remainder. See §§ 3.5, 3.6.

system is an estate in fee simple defeasible.[10]

TRADITIONAL SYSTEM	*SIMPLIFIED SYSTEM*
Fee simple determinable	Fee simple defeasible
Fee simple subject to a condition subsequent	Fee simple defeasible
Fee simple subject to an executory limitation	Fee simple defeasible

§ 2.5   The Fee Tail

The estate in *fee tail*—created by language such as "to *A* and the heirs of his body"—is subject to termination upon the death of the tenant in tail's last living descendant.

---

[10] As we shall see in the materials on future interests (§§ 3.3, 3.6), the Restatement 3d of Property also rewrites the distinctions among the three future interests following a defeasible fee—the possibility of reverter, the right of entry, the executory interest—by labeling the future interest as either a "reversion" or a "remainder."

The fee tail estate has an interesting history, designed to preserve wealth within the great English landed families, but its present is no longer very important and its future even less so. In almost all American jurisdictions, the fee tail estate has been abolished. Language purporting to create it—"to *A* and the heirs of his body"—has different consequences in different states. The most predominant results are that it creates a fee simple absolute in *A*, or that it creates a life estate in *A* with a remainder in *A*'s lineal descendants.

The Restatement 3d of Property articulates the position of the American Law Institute in proclaiming that "[t]he fee tail estate is not recognized in American law. A disposition 'to *A* and the heirs of *A*'s body' or the like creates a fee simple absolute in *A*. A disposition 'to *A* for life, then to the heirs of *A*'s body' or the like creates a life estate in *A* followed by a future interest in fee simple absolute in *A*'s issue who would take from *A* under the applicable statute of intestacy." Restatement 3d of Property § 24.4.

§ 2.6 Life Estates

Life estates are estates that expire naturally (by their own terms) on the death of the governing life.

In most cases, the governing life is the life tenant.

> *Example 2.6:* G conveyed land "to *A* for life."
>
> *A* has a life estate. The same would be true if the grant had been "to *A* so long as *A* lives," "to *A* until *A*'s death," or "to *A* during *A*'s lifetime."[11]

The phrase *equitable life estate* is sometimes used to describe the interest of a trust beneficiary who has the right to the income from a trust for his or her lifetime.

By adding a special limitation or a condition subsequent to the grant, life estates can be made prematurely defeasible, so that they might end before the life tenant's death.

---

[11]The future interest retained by *G* is known, in both the traditional and simplified systems of classification, as a reversion. See §§ 3.2, 3.3.

TRADITIONAL SYSTEM	*SIMPLIFIED SYSTEM*
Determinable life estate, or Life estate subject to a special limitation	Defeasible life estate
Life estate subject to a condition subsequent	Defeasible life estate
Life estate subject to an executory limitation	Defeasible life estate

Example 2.7: G conveyed land "to *A* for life or until *A* remarries."

In the traditional system of classification, *A*'s estate is called a life estate subject to a special limitation or a determinable life estate. In the simplified system of the Restatement 3d of Property, *A*'s estate is a defeasible life estate.[12]

---

[12]In the traditional system of classification, the future interest retained by *G* is a reversion, which takes effect on the earlier of *A*'s death or remarriage. Some scholars have said that *G*'s interest that may take effect on *A*'s remarriage is a possibility of reverter, but such scholars disagree on whether the possibility of reverter merges into the reversion. The

Example 2.8: (1) *G* conveyed land "to *A* for life, remainder to *B*; but if *A* remarries, to *B* immediately." In the traditional system of classification, *A*'s estate is called a life estate subject to an executory limitation. In the simplified system of the Restatement 3d of Property, *A*'s estate is a defeasible life estate.[13]

(2) *G* conveyed land "to *A* for life on condition that *A* not remarry, but if *A* remarries, the grantor has the right to re-enter and take possession." In the traditional system of classification, *A*'s estate is called a life estate

better view is that *G* retained only a reversion. The reason is that *G* transferred out an estate of lesser quantum than *G* originally possessed. See the definition of a reversion in § 3.2.

In the simplified system of classification, the future interest retained by *G* is a reversion.

[13]In the traditional system of classification, *B* has both a remainder and an executory interest. The remainder takes effect in possession on *A*'s death if *A* never remarries. If *A* remarries, the executory interest takes effect in possession on the remarriage. In the simplified system of classification, both of these interests are called remainders—and it would be best to say that *B* has only one interest, a remainder, that will take effect in possession on the earlier of *A*'s remarriage or death. For the classification of these future interests, see §§ 3.4-3.6.

subject to a condition subsequent. In the simplified system of the Restatement 3d of Property, *A*'s estate is a defeasible life estate.[14]

A life estate customarily arises from the inclusion of words expressly limiting the duration of the estate to a lifetime ("to *A for life*"). But a life estate can also be indicated implicitly. Consider the following example.

Example 2.9: G conveyed land "to *A* so long as he occupies the land."

Most decisions hold that *A* has a life estate subject to a special limitation, not a fee simple determinable, because *A*'s ability to occupy the land ends at *A*'s death. See Restatement of

[14]In the traditional system of classification, *G* has both a reversion and a right of entry. The reversion takes effect in possession on *A*'s death if *A* never remarries. If *A* remarries, the right of entry permits *G* to divest *A* of the remaining portion of the life estate. In the simplified system of classification, both of these interests are called reversions—and it would be best to say that *G* has only one interest, a reversion, that will take effect in possession on the earlier of *A*'s remarriage or death. For the classification of these future interests, see §§ 3.2, 3.3.

Property § 112 illus. 2.[15] This life estate subject to a special limitation is known in the simplified system of the Restatement 3d of Property as a defeasible life estate.

A life estate need not be measured by the life of the one in possession, but can be measured by the life of another. This type of estate is traditionally called a *life estate pur autre vie*. The Restatement 3d of Property translates the law French into English: a *life estate for the life of another*.

TRADITIONAL SYSTEM	*SIMPLIFIED SYSTEM*
Life estate pur autre vie	Life estate for the life of another

Example 2.10: G conveyed land "to *A* for the life of *B*." *A* predeceases *B*. *A*'s will devises her entire estate to *X*.

A has a life estate pur autre vie or a life estate for the life of another. Unlike a life estate

---

[15]In both the traditional and simplified systems of classification, the future interest retained by *G* is a reversion. See §§ 3.2, 3.3.

that terminates on the life tenant's death, *A* can devise the remaining portion of her life estate to *X*. After *A*'s death, *X* has a life estate pur autre vie or a life estate for the life of another—for the life of *B*.[16]

§ 2.7 Terms of Years

Terms of years are estates that expire naturally (by their own terms) on the expiration of the term. Terms of years are defeasible estates because they are subject to a limitation ("to *A* for 10 years" or "to *A* for 30 days").

By adding a special limitation or a condition subsequent to the grant, terms of years can be made prematurely defeasible, so that they might end before the expiration of the term.

Example 2.11: G conveyed land "to *A* for 10 years or until *A* remarries."

In the traditional system of classification, *A*'s estate is called a term of years subject to a special limitation or a determinable term of years. In the simplified system of the

---

[16]In both the traditional and simplified systems of classification, the future interest retained by *G* is a reversion. See §§ 3.2, 3.3.

Restatement 3d of Property, A's estate is a defeasible term of years.[17]

Because a term of years is a nonfreehold estate (see § 2.2), a grant "to *A* for 10 years, then to *B*" was not characterized at common law as a term of years in *A* followed by a remainder in *B*. Rather, *B* was characterized as owning the land in fee simple absolute subject to *A*'s term of years. Today, the distinction between freehold and nonfreehold estates has little continuing importance. Characterizing *B* as owning the land subject to a term of years in *A* may still be appropriate in a commercial transaction, such as where *B*, as landlord, leases the land to *A*, as tenant. In the setting of noncommercial transactions, however, the ancient characterization was abolished in the Restatement of Property § 156 cmt. e, which states in pertinent part: "The creation of a remainder in land does not require ... that the estates preceding the future interest be freehold estates." This *Nutshell* follows the modern usage as described in the Restatement.

[17]In both the traditional and simplified systems of classification, the future interest retained by *G* is a reversion. See §§ 3.2, 3.3.

§ 2.8   Estates from Period to Period, at Will, or at Sufferance

These estates have little importance outside the context of landlord and tenant, and can be briefly summarized. An *estate from period to period* is "an estate which will continue for successive periods of a year, or successive periods of a fraction of a year, unless it is terminated." Restatement of Property § 20. An *estate at will* is "an estate which is terminable at the will of the transferor and also at the will of the transferee and which has no other designated period of duration." *Id.* at § 21. An *estate at sufferance* is "an interest in land which exists when a person who had a possessory interest in land by virtue of an effective conveyance, wrongfully continues in the possession of the land after the termination of such interest, but without asserting a claim to a superior title." *Id.* at § 22.

CHAPTER 3

CLASSIFYING FUTURE INTERESTS

§ 3.1 The Distinction Between Reversionary and Nonreversionary Future Interests

The first step in the process of classification of future interests is to decide whether the future interest is a reversionary interest or a nonreversionary interest. Three of the five future interests within the traditional system of classification are reversionary interests: the reversion, the possibility of reverter, and the right of entry. The other two future interests within the traditional system of classification—the remainder and the executory interest—are nonreversionary.

REVERSIONARY FUTURE INTERESTS	*NONREVERSIONARY FUTURE INTERESTS*
Reversion	Remainder
Possibility of reverter	Executory interest
Right of entry	

The following rules will help you understand the distinction between reversionary and nonreversionary interests.

☞ *Rule 1: To be* REVERSIONARY, *a future interest must be retained by (or created in) the transferor.*

☞ *Rule 2: To be* NONREVERSIONARY, *a future interest must be created in a transferee (someone other than the transferor).*

Once made, a classification based on the reversionary/nonreversionary distinction is not altered by subsequent transfers of the interest from one person to another. So, a reversionary interest does not become nonreversionary by virtue of a subsequent transfer of that interest from the transferor to a transferee. And, conversely, a nonreversionary interest does not become reversionary if it subsequently comes into the hands of the transferor. It makes no difference whether the subsequent transfer is inter vivos, testamentary, or the result of intestate succession.

Example 3.1: G conveyed land "to A for life." Later, but while A was alive, G conveyed all his remaining interest in the land to B.

B's interest is reversionary. When G made the second conveyance, he no longer owned the life estate he had previously conveyed to A; G owned only a reversionary interest. The second conveyance transferred this reversionary interest to B.

Example 3.2: G conveyed land "to A for life." G later died leaving a will that did not mention the land but contained a residuary clause devising all his property not otherwise disposed of to B. G was survived by A and B.

Same result as in Example 3.1. The fact that the second conveyance occurred at G's death rather than during G's lifetime makes no difference.

Example 3.3: G conveyed land "to A for life." G later died intestate, i.e., without a valid will. G was survived by A and by his sole heir, B.

Same result. The fact that the conveyance to B occurred by operation of law (the intestacy statute) rather than by inter vivos conveyance or by will makes no difference.

Distinguishing a reversionary interest from a nonreversionary interest is easy if the interest was originally created during the transferor's lifetime, as in the examples above. When G carved out and conveyed a life estate to A, G retained what he did not transfer—a reversionary interest.

If G still owned the property in fee simple at his death, however, and devised a life estate in the property to A at that time, would the future interest be originally created in G or in a transferee? Common sense suggests that a dead transferor cannot retain anything. Yet the law views the situation differently. If A's life estate was created in G's will, the nature of the future interest depends on whether it also passed under G's will or whether it passed to G's heirs by intestacy.

Example 3.4: G's will devised land "to A for life." G's will contained no residuary clause devising property not otherwise mentioned. Thus the rest of G's property passed by intestacy to G's sole heir, B.

B's interest is reversionary, because it did not pass to *B* by the same instrument as *A*'s interest.

Example 3.5: *G*'s will devised land "to *A* for life" and devised the residue of his estate to *B*.

Most courts and authorities would say that *B*'s interest is nonreversionary, because it was created in *B* at the same time and by the same instrument (albeit not the same part of the instrument) as *A*'s life estate.

Example 3.6: *G*'s will devised land "to *A* for life, and upon *A*'s death, the land goes to *B*."

B's interest is clearly nonreversionary, because it was created in *B* at the same time and by the same part of the instrument (indeed, the same clause) as *A*'s life estate.

§ 3.2 Reversionary Interests Under the Traditional System of Classification: Reversions, Reverters, Rights of Entry

Under the traditional system of classification, if a future interest is reversionary, it is a reversion, a possibility of reverter, or a right of entry.

How do you differentiate among reversions, possibilities of reverter, and rights of entry?

☞ *REVERSIONS are future interests retained by transferors when they transfer out an estate or estates of less quantum than they originally had.*

Because a particular estate (a possessory estate other than a fee simple) is an estate of less quantum than a fee simple estate (see § 2.2), a property owner retains a reversion when the owner transfers out a particular estate and (1) does not create a nonreversionary future interest to follow it or (2) creates one or more nonreversionary future interests that do not exhaust all possible post-transfer events.

☞ *POSSIBILITIES OF REVERTER are future interests retained by transferors when they transfer out an estate or estates of the same quantum as they originally had.*

Because all fee simple estates are of the same quantum (see § 2.2), a property owner retains a possibility of reverter when the owner transfers out a fee simple determinable and (1) does not create an executory interest or (2) creates one or more executory interests that do not exhaust all possible post-transfer events.

☞ *RIGHTS OF ENTRY*[1] *are future interests created in transferors when they transfer out an estate subject to a condition subsequent (i.e., subject to divestment).*

Whether the quantum of the estate is the same as or lesser than that of the transferor's original estate is unimportant. The most common example is that of an owner of property in fee simple absolute who transfers out a fee simple subject to a condition subsequent, who expressly creates in himself or herself a right to re-enter and retake the premises if and when the condition is broken, and who (1) does not create an executory interest or (2) creates one or more executory interests that do not exhaust all possible post-transfer events.

§ 3.2.1 Reversionary interests where no future interest created

We are now ready to illustrate each of the reversionary future interests.

Example 3.7: G conveyed land "to *A* for life."
Or, *G* conveyed land "to *A* for 10 years."

---

[1]Rights of entry go by other names: rights of re-entry, rights of entry for condition broken, powers of termination. The terms are interchangeable.

G retained a reversionary interest, and the traditional system of classification calls that reversionary interest a reversion. Note that *G*'s reversion was not expressly stated but rather arose because *G* transferred an estate of less quantum than *G* owned (a particular estate is an estate of less quantum than a fee simple estate) and therefore retained what was not conveyed. It would not change the analysis if *G*'s reversion had been expressly stated. For example, if the first conveyance had said "to *A* for life, and upon *A*'s death, to return to me," G would still have retained a reversion.

Example 3.8: G conveyed land "to *A* and his heirs so long as *A* does not allow liquor to be sold on the premises[, and upon *A*'s allowing liquor to be sold on the premises, the property is to revert to the grantor]."

G retained a reversionary interest, and the traditional system of classification calls that reversionary interest a possibility of reverter.

The words contained in brackets in the preceding example are not necessary to create a possibility of reverter. Possibilities of reverter need not be expressly stated because, like reversions, they constitute an undisposed-of interest remaining in the transferor. See Simes & Smith on Future Interests § 286. In practice, however, it is common expressly to state the possibility of reverter, and a small minority of decisions has held (erroneously) that, without the bracketed words, *A* takes a fee simple absolute. See, e.g., *In re Copps Chapel Methodist Episcopal Church*, 120 Ohio St. 309, 166 N.E. 218 (1929).

> *Example 3.9:* *G* conveyed land "to *A* and his heirs on condition that *A* not allow liquor to be sold on the premises[, but if *A* allows liquor to be sold on the premises, the grantor is to have the right to re-enter and take possession of the premises]."
>
> *G* retained (more accurately, created in himself) a reversionary interest, and the traditional system of classification calls that reversionary interest a right of entry.

The right of entry is different from other future interests in the following sense. The right of entry does not take effect in possession automatically when the condition is broken. If *A* allows liquor to be sold on the premises, *A*'s action merely gives *G* a right to elect to take a possessory interest if *G* so chooses. But this difference between rights of entry and other interests (for example, the possibility of reverter) has little practical importance in the modern era. The early common-law rule was that a right of entry could be exercised only by a physical entry on the land. In most states today, however, the commencement of an action to regain possession satisfies the requirement of an election to divest the possessory estate, and the holder of a possibility of reverter often must institute a similar action in order to enforce his or her "automatic" interest. In addition, after the stipulated event has occurred, the time allowable under the law of many states for making an election under a right of entry is the same as that for bringing an action to enforce a possibility of reverter. The two possessory interests may thus be more in alignment than one would think.

There is another feature distinguishing rights of entry from reversions and possibilities of reverter. A right of entry is not the undisposed-of interest retained by the transferor when she transfers out other interests. Rather, it is a newly created future interest in the transferor. Does this mean that a right of entry must be expressly created? Theoretically, no. The transfer of a fee simple subject to a condition subsequent *by itself* causes a right of entry to arise in the grantor. Thus, in Example 3.9, omission of the bracketed portions of the disposition would not necessarily prevent *G* from having a right of entry. Simes and Smith on Future Interests § 247. On the other hand, the law recognizes a strong constructional preference against forfeitures (in this example, against *A* forfeiting *A*'s present estate). It is possible, and perhaps even likely, that the omission of the bracketed portions would result in a court concluding that *G* had not intended to retain a right of entry. For further discussion see § 3.2.4.

§ 3.2.2   Reversionary interests where one or more future interests were created

We are now ready to look at a few examples in which the transferor created one or more future interests in transferees. There will still be a reversionary future interest if all possible post-transfer events have not been exhausted by the contingencies attached to these nonreversionary future interests.

Example 3.10: G transferred land "to *A* for life, then to *B* if *B* survives *A*."

G retained a reversionary interest, because *B*'s interest is subject to a condition precedent of survival (which might or might not be satisfied), and the transfer does not provide for any other transferee to receive the property if *B* fails to survive. In the traditional system of classification, *G*'s reversionary interest is a reversion, because the only vested estate in the sequence (*A*'s life estate) is of less quantum than *G*'s original fee simple absolute. (The terms "condition precedent" and "vested" are explained in § 3.8.)

Example 3.11: *G* transferred land "to *A* for life, then to *B* if *B* survives *A*, but if not, to *C* if *C* survives *A*."

G retained a reversionary interest, because *B*'s interest and *C*'s interest are each subject to a condition precedent of survival (which might or might not be satisfied), and the transfer does not provide for any other transferee to receive the property if both *B* and *C* fail to survive *A*. In the traditional system of classification, *G*'s reversionary interest is a reversion, because the only vested estate in the sequence (*A*'s life estate) is of less quantum than *G*'s original fee simple absolute.

Example 3.12: G transferred land "to A and his heirs as long as A does not allow liquor to be sold on the land, and upon A's allowing liquor to be sold on the land, the land is to go to B if B is then living, and if B is not then living, to C if C is then living, and if neither B nor C is then living, the land is to revert to the grantor."

G retained a reversionary interest, because B's interest and C's interest are each subject to a condition precedent of survival (which might or might not be satisfied). In the traditional system of classification, G's reversionary interest is a possibility of reverter because the only vested estate in the sequence (A's fee simple determinable) is of the same quantum as G's original fee simple absolute.

A much rarer example of the possibility of reverter can be illustrated by a variation on Example 3.10.

Example 3.13: G conveyed land "to A for life, then to B, but if B fails to survive A, the property is to return to me."

G retained a reversionary interest, because B's interest is subject to a condition of survival (which might or might not be satisfied), and the conveyance does not provide for any other transferee to receive the property if *B* fails to survive. *G*'s reversionary interest is classified as a possibility of reverter, not a remainder. The condition of survival is a condition subsequent, rendering *B*'s interest vested. (For elaboration, see § 3.8.2.) *G* has thus conveyed out two vested interests, unlike in Example 3.10: *A*'s life estate and *B*'s remainder, which together are in effect a fee simple. The sum of these two vested interests yields an estate of the same quantum as *G* originally owned. Accordingly, *G*'s retained interest is classified in the traditional system as a possibility of reverter. Restatement of Property § 154 cmt. e & illus. 2; Am. L. Prop. § 4.18.

§ 3.2.3 Reversionary future interests following particular estates subject to premature termination

Sections 2.6 and 2.7 explained that a life estate or term of years may be subjected to possible termination before the life tenant's death or the expiration of the term. This additional event may be stated either in the form of a limitation or in the form of a condition subsequent. In either case, the transferor has a reversionary future interest called, in the traditional system of classification, a reversion. Consider the following example.

Example 3.14: G transferred land "to A for life on condition that A not remarry, but if A remarries, the grantor has the right to re-enter and take possession."

G has both a right of entry and a reversion. The reversion takes effect in possession on A's death if A never remarries. If A remarries, the right of entry permits G to divest A of the remaining portion of the life estate.

If the additional event is expressed as a limitation, the particular estate is called a life estate (or term of years) subject to a special limitation. By the better view, the transferor has not retained a possibility of reverter in addition to the reversion.

Example 3.15: G transferred land "to A for life or until A remarries."

G has only a reversion, which takes effect in possession on the earlier of A's death or remarriage. The reason is that G transferred an estate of lesser quantum than G originally had. Thus G's interest fits the definition of a reversion. A possibility of reverter properly arises only when G transfers an estate of the same quantum as *G* originally owned. In this example, *G* transferred a life estate. A life estate, whether or not subject to a special limitation, is an estate of lesser quantum than a fee simple.

§ 3.2.4 Ambiguous language: Possibility of reverter or right of entry?

The dispositive language in Examples 3.8 and 3.9 is unambiguous. Language granting *A* a fee simple determinable is followed by language describing a possibility of reverter; language granting *A* a fee simple subject to a condition subsequent is followed by language describing a right of entry.

In practice, unfortunately, the language of an actual disposition may be ambiguous. In such cases, courts often assert that forfeitures of present estates are disfavored in the law. Thus, a forfeiture will be avoided entirely if the language admits of some other construction and, if not, then at least the optional forfeiture incident to a right of entry will be preferred to the "automatic" forfeiture incident to a possibility of reverter. These constructional preferences gain strength as the amount of consideration paid by the grantee rises in relation to the value of a fee simple absolute in the land at the time of the grant. Nevertheless, these are tendencies only, and the result reached in any given case may be unpredictable. To avoid litigation, lawyers should be careful to use standard language, clearly coupling reverters with limitations, and rights of entry with conditions.

When litigation arises, cases of ambiguous language frequently fall into one of five categories.

First, the transfer may combine words of condition with a reverter clause ("to *A* and his heirs on condition that *A* never allow liquor to be sold, but if *A* allows liquor to be sold, the property is to revert to me"). Under the structure of estates, of course, a possibility of reverter can only follow a fee simple determinable, not a fee simple subject to a condition subsequent. Some courts resolve the contradiction by holding that the reverter language in the second clause means that the grantor intended to convey a fee simple determinable in the first clause. However, the Restatement of Property § 45 cmt m. and some other courts take the opposite view: the language of condition in the first clause is controlling and manifests an intention to retain only a right of entry. Still other courts reach the Restatement's conclusion by preferring the less drastic forfeiture of a right of entry over the "automatic" forfeiture of the possibility of reverter.

Second, the transfer may contain a statement of purpose plus a reverter clause (a transfer of land to a school district "to be used for school purposes and ceasing to be used for school purposes, it shall revert to the grantor"). Cases interpreting such clauses are split. Some hold that the unambiguous reverter language in the second clause means that the grantor intended to convey a fee simple determinable in the first clause. Others hold that the grantor retained only a right of entry; these latter cases often invoke the constructional preference against automatic forfeiture.

Third, the transfer may contain only a statement of purpose (a transfer of land to a school district "for school purposes"). The predominant result in such cases is to hold that the possessory estate is a fee simple absolute, with nothing retained by the grantor. See Restatement of Property § 45 cmt. o; *Town of Nahant v. United States*, 293 F. Supp. 1076 (D.Mass. 1968).

Fourth, the transfer may contain only words of limitation ("to the school district so long as used for school purposes"). The most likely result in such cases is to hold that a fee simple determinable was created in the transferee, leaving a possibility of reverter in the grantor.

Fifth and last, the transfer may contain only words of condition (to the grantee "on condition that the premises shall never be used as a tavern"). In the absence of an express right of entry, courts tend not to construe the estate as a fee simple subject to a condition subsequent. Instead, courts tend to construe the estate as a fee simple absolute: perhaps subject to a contractual obligation in favor of the grantor (a covenant restricting the use of the land); or perhaps subject to a trust obligation in favor of the grantor (a result especially likely when the grant was for a charitable purpose); or perhaps subject to an equitable charge or lien (a result likely if the condition requires the transferee to pay a sum of money to one or more third parties); or perhaps with no enforceable obligation at all. This last option renders the language in the grant merely an expression of the grantor's motives or purposes.

All of this discussion serves as a reminder of the drafting point made earlier: lawyers should be careful to use the language of estates and future interests clearly and correctly, so that courts do not have to guess the transferor's intention.

§ 3.2.5 Some legal incidents of possibilities of reverter and rights of entry

Enforcement. A fee simple determinable terminates automatically if and when the terminating event happens; the right to possession is instantly shifted to the holder of the possibility of reverter. Possibilities of reverter become possessory automatically upon the happening of the terminating event.

In the case of a right of entry, however, the rule is different: Rights of entry do not automatically become possessory if and when the specified event happens; the right to possession arises upon the grantor's later exercise of the right to re-enter (or upon exercise by the grantor's successors in interest, as described below). In other words, the happening of the specified event does not divest the possessory estate; it merely authorizes the grantor or the grantor's successors to divest the possessory estate.

The above difference between possibilities of reverter and rights of entry, while theoretically valid, may have less practical importance than it may seem. The early common-law rule was that a right of entry could be exercised only by a physical entry on the land. In most states now, however, the commencement of an action to regain possession satisfies the requirement of an election to divest the possessory estate, and the holder of a possibility of reverter often must institute a similar action in order to enforce his or her "automatic" interest. In addition, after the stipulated event has occurred, the time allowable under the law of many states for bringing an action to enforce a possibility of reverter is the same as that for making an election under a right of entry. The statute of limitations in several states explicitly begins running upon the occurrence of the specified event against both a possibility of reverter and a right of entry; in other states the statute has been so interpreted; and in still others, the statute is open to such an interpretation. The two interests may thus be in alignment on the question of adverse possession. Finally, although the statute of limitations in some states is held not to begin running until an election under a right of entry has been made, the courts, drawing an analogy to the equitable doctrine of laches, have required that an election be made within a "reasonable time" after the breach of the condition; and there is authority that the limitations period constitutes a "reasonable time."

The Rule Against Perpetuities and Statutory Restrictions on Duration. It is assumed that possibilities of reverter and rights of entry, probably for mostly historical reasons, are exempt from the Rule Against Perpetuities, and all American courts that have decided the question have so held. It should be noted, however, that in many states the question has not been decided.

In response to the inapplicability or supposed inapplicability of the Rule Against Perpetuities to these interests, a few states have statutes that impose a cut off of possibilities of reverter and rights of entry after a certain period of time. The statutes vary in detail, but they generally state that these interests cease to exist if the event upon which they are predicated has not occurred within a certain period of time—ranging from thirty to sixty years. The effect of their ceasing to exist is to render the possessory estate *absolute*, whether it was a fee simple determinable or a fee simple subject to a condition subsequent. For a more detailed discussion of these statutes, see T.P. Gallanis, The Future of Future Interests, 60 Wash. & Lee L. Rev. 513, 558-559 (2003).

§ 3.3   Reversionary Interests   Under the Restatement 3d of Property

The simplified system of classification in the Restatement 3d of Property eliminates the distinctions among reversions, possibilities of reverter, and rights of entry. All reversionary interests are called *reversions*. Section 25.2 of the Restatement 3d of Property states: "A future interest is either a reversion or a remainder. A future interest is a reversion if it was retained by the transferor. A future interest is a remainder if it was created in a transferee."

Under the simplified system of classification, *G*'s interest in Examples 3.7 through 3.15, above, is a *reversion*.

TRADITIONAL SYSTEM	*SIMPLIFIED SYSTEM*
Reversion	Reversion
Possibility of reverter	Reversion
Right of entry	Reversion

We now turn from reversionary interests to nonreversionary interests.

§ 3.4 Remainders Under the Traditional System of Classification

The one nonreversionary interest permitted at common law before the Statute of Uses (on which, see the next section) was the remainder.[2] A remainder, as traditionally defined, is a future interest created in a transferee that becomes possessory if at all upon the natural termination of the preceding interest. The preceding interest (1) must have been created simultaneously with the creation of the future interest and (2) must be a particular estate. Recall that a particular estate is a term of art denoting any possessory interest other than a fee simple interest.

Example 3.16: (1) G transferred land "to *A* for life, and upon *A*'s death, to *B*."

(2) G transferred land "to *A* for 10 years, and at the expiration thereof, to *B*."

B has a remainder. (With respect to Variation (2), recall the discussion after Example 2.11.)

---

[2]The term "remainder" was derived from the idea of an interest that "remained out" after the termination of a prior estate.

Example 3.17: (1) G transferred land "to *A* for life or until *A* remarries, and upon *A*'s death or remarriage, to *B*."

(2) G transferred land "to *A* for 10 years or until *A*'s remarriage, whichever sooner occurs, and upon the expiration of 10 years or *A*'s earlier remarriage, to *B*."

Technically, *B* has two interests, both remainders. But it is common to say simply that *B* has a remainder.

§ 3.5   The Statute of Uses and Executory Interests

The Statute of Uses, enacted in 1535 and effective in 1536, made possible a new nonreversionary future interest, called the executory interest. To understand the executory interest, you will need some brief historical background.

For much of its history, England had multiple, often overlapping systems of courts. Some courts were known as courts of common law, because their decisions created and enforced the common law. In addition, there was the Court of Chancery, headed by a senior royal official known as the Chancellor. The Chancellor was not bound by the rules of common law but instead was able to render decisions that took into account the justice or fairness of the parties' particular facts. The system of law administered by the Court of Chancery was known as equity.

Some property interests not recognized at common law were protected by the Court of Chancery. Consider the following example.

Example 3.18: G transferred land "to T for T to hold, so that the property may be used by A for life, then by B."

From the perspective of the common law, the owner of the land was T. T had legal title, meaning title enforceable at common law. Where did that leave A and B? As far as the common law was concerned, A and B had no rights in the land. But A and B could go to the Court of Chancery, which recognized that the purpose of the transfer was to benefit A and B, not T. From the perspective of the Chancellor, T was merely a kind of trustee, holding the land for A and B. T might have the legal title, but it was A and B who had title in equity.

Why did G create this kind of transfer? The answer was (1) to avoid some then-existing forms of taxation, which would apply only to legal, not equitable, interests, and (2) to avoid medieval rules prohibiting the transfer of land by will.

The Statute of Uses was designed to stop this evasion. It stated in pertinent part: "[W]here any such person ... be seised ... in any lands ... to the use ... of any other person[,]... in every such case ... every such person ... that have ... any such use ... shall ... henceforth ... be seised ...." In other words, the statute transferred the legally recognized interests to the people who previously held only the use. Applying the Statute of Uses to Example 3.18: *A* holds a legal life estate, *B* holds a legal remainder, and *T* takes nothing.

The Statute of Uses had additional consequences. One of these was to permit the creation of a type of nonreversionary future interest that could not have been created at common law. Consider a variation on Example 3.9.

Example 3.19: *G* conveyed land "to *A* and his heirs on condition that *A* not allow liquor to be sold on the premises, but if *A* allows liquor to be sold on the premises, the land is to go to *B*."

In this example, *G* wants the sale of alcohol to trigger, not a right of entry, but instead a transfer of the property to *B*. This result could not be accomplished at common law, which permitted defeasible fees to be followed only by reversionary interests, not by nonreversionary interests. After the Statute of Uses, however, *G* can achieve the desired result, as illustrated in the following example.

Example 3.20: *G* conveyed land "to *T* for the use of *A* and his heirs on condition that *A* not allow liquor to be sold on the premises, but if *A* allows liquor to be sold on the premises, the property is to be for the use of *B*."

The Statute of Uses created legally-recognized interests in *A* and *B*. Over time, these interests became accepted even without the intermediate transfer to *T*. Each of the interests has a name: *B*'s future interest is traditionally called an *executory interest*; *A*'s present estate is traditionally called a *fee simple subject to an executory limitation*.

The Statute of Uses also had the effect of permitting nonreversionary interests to follow the fee simple determinable. These interests are also traditionally called executory interests.

Example 3.21: *G* transferred land "to *A* and his heirs so long as *A* does not allow liquor to be sold on the premises, and upon *A*'s allowing liquor to be sold on the premises, to *B*."

After the Statute of Uses, *B* has an executory interest.

One can also create executory interests following estates less than fee simple.

Example 3.22: (1) G transferred land "to *A* for life, and upon *A*'s death, to *B*; but if *A* remarries, the land goes to *B* immediately."

(2) G transferred land "to *A* for 10 years, and at the expiration thereof, to *B*; but if during the 10-year period *A* remarries, the land goes to *B* immediately."

Under the traditional system of classification, *B* has both an executory interest and a remainder. The executory interest takes effect in possession if *A* remarries. The remainder takes effect in possession if *A* does not remarry. (On Variation (2), recall the discussion after Example 2.11.)

Executory interests are traditionally divided into two categories—springing and shifting. *Shifting* executory interests potentially divest an interest conferred by the grantor on a transferee. *Springing* executory interests potentially divest an interest retained by the grantor.

Example 3.23: (1) G transferred land "to *A* and his heirs, but if *A* allows liquor to be sold on the premises, to *B*."

(2) G transferred land "to *B* and his heirs, to take effect in possession on *B*'s future marriage."

B's executory interest is *shifting* in Variation (1) and *springing* in Variation (2).

§ 3.6 Nonreversionary Interests Under the Restatement 3d of Property

The simplified system of classification in the Restatement 3d of Property eliminates the distinction between remainders and executory interests. All nonreversionary interests are called *remainders*. Section 25.2 of the Restatement 3d of Property states:

> A future interest is either a reversion or a remainder. A future interest is a reversion if it was retained by the transferor. A future interest is a remainder if it was created in a transferee.

Under the simplified system of classification, *B*'s interest in Examples 3.16 through 3.23, above, is a remainder.

TRADITIONAL SYSTEM	*SIMPLIFIED SYSTEM*
Remainder	Remainder
Executory interest	Remainder

§ 3.7   Should the Restatement 3d of Property Have Eliminated the Distinction Between Reversions and Remainders?

The authors of the Restatement 3d of Property considered whether to eliminate the distinction between reversions and remainders. The authors recognize that, under the Restatement system, "[n]o legal consequences in property law attach to the choice of labels, because there is no longer any persuasive reason for continuing to recognize the distinction between reversionary and nonreversionary interests." Restatement 3d of Property § 25.2 cmt. e. However, the distinction is retained in the Restatement in order to comport with the customary vocabulary of the legal profession and with current Restatements and uniform laws:

> The reason for categorizing future interests as either reversions or remainders is that the

legal profession, especially in describing future interests created in a trust, is accustomed to referring to a future interest retained by the transferor as a "reversion" and a future interest created in a transferee as a "remainder." In addition, the Restatement Third of Trusts refers to a resulting trust as a "reversionary, equitable interest" (see Restatement Third, Trusts § 7), and the Restatement Third of Trusts and the Restatement Third of Restitution variously refer to property as "reverting" or "reverting back" to the transferor or the transferor's estate or successors in interest in certain cases. Finally, various uniform statutes, such as the Uniform Trust Code and the Uniform Principal and Income Act, refer to the future interest in trust principal as a "remainder."

Restatement 3d of Property § 25.2 cmt. e. See also Restatement 3d of Property § 25.2 Reporter's Note, observing that "[c]ertain concepts in tax law do depend on the distinction" between reversions and remainders.

§ 3.8 Classification in Terms of Vesting Under the Traditional System

Future interests are subject to a further level of classification—classification in terms of vesting. Under the traditional system of classification, there are four categories here: indefeasibly vested, vested subject to (complete) defeasance, vested subject to open (partial defeasance), and contingent (nonvested).

§ 3.8.1 Indefeasibly vested

An *indefeasibly vested* future interest is one that is not subject to any conditions or limitations. In other words, the future interest must be certain to become a possessory fee simple absolute at some time in the future. Only remainders and reversions can be indefeasibly vested.

Example 3.24: G transferred land "to A for life, remainder to B."

B's remainder is indefeasibly vested. It is certain to become possessory because A is bound to die. When A dies, B's remainder will become a possessory fee simple absolute.

Note in this example that B might not be alive when A dies. Except as otherwise provided by statute, B's interest is not subject to a condition of survival of *A*. Therefore, the possibility of *B*'s death before *A*'s death has no bearing on the classification of *B*'s interest. If *B* dies before *A*, *B*'s indefeasibly vested remainder will pass at *B*'s death to *B*'s successors in interest—her devisees or, if she dies intestate, her heirs.

Example 3.25: *G* conveyed land "to *A* for life."

G's reversion is indefeasibly vested. The comments made in the previous example regarding *B*'s remainder apply to *G*'s reversion in this example.

Example 3.26: *G* conveyed land "to *A* for life, remainder to *B* for 10 years."

G's reversion is indefeasibly vested. It is certain to become possessory 10 years after *A*'s death, and will at that time become a fee simple absolute.

B's remainder is not indefeasibly vested. Although it is certain to become possessory upon *A*'s death (a certain event), it will not become a fee simple absolute then. *B*'s remainder is vested subject to defeasance after 10 years. The comments made in Example 3.24 regarding survival apply equally here.

§ 3.8.2   Vested subject to defeasance

Under the traditional system of classification, a future interest that is *vested subject to defeasance* is one that is subject to one or more conditions subsequent or to one or more limitations. The precise terminology to be used will depend on whether the interest is subject to conditions subsequent, on the one hand, or to limitations, on the other hand. (Recall the definitions of these terms in § 2.4.)

If the future interest is subject to one or more *conditions subsequent*, it is called *vested subject to divestment*. Only remainders and reversions can be vested subject to divestment. Note, however, that there is an important difference between remainders and reversions. Remainders are vested subject to divestment only when they are subject to a condition subsequent. (As we shall shortly see, remainders subject to a condition precedent are contingent.) In contrast, reversions are vested subject to divestment whenever they are subject to a condition, regardless of whether the condition is precedent or subsequent. The reason for this difference is that, by definitional fiat under the traditional system of classification, reversions can never be contingent. *Reversions under the traditional system of classification are always vested.*

Example 3.27: G transferred land "to A for life, remainder to B, but if B fails to survive A, to C."

B's remainder is vested subject to divestment because the condition of survival attached to her remainder is stated in condition subsequent form—"to B, but if."

C's executory interest is subject to the condition that B not survive A. From C's perspective, the condition is stated in the form of a condition precedent—"if...to C." Thus, C's executory interest is contingent.

Example 3.28: G conveyed land "to A for life, remainder to B if B survives A, but if not, to return to me."

B's remainder is subject to a condition of survival of A, but this time the condition is stated in the form of a condition precedent—"to B if." B's remainder is therefore contingent, not vested subject to divestment.

G's reversion is subject to the condition that B not survive A. From G's perspective, the condition is a condition precedent—"if...to return to me." This indicates that G's reversion should be classified as contingent. However, the rule that reversions are always vested overrides all other rules. Thus, *G*'s reversion is vested subject to divestment.

Example 3.29: *G* conveyed land "to *A* for life, remainder to *B* if *B* survives *A*, but if not, to *C*."

B's remainder is subject to a condition of survival of *A* that is stated in the form of a condition precedent—"to *B* if." *B*'s remainder is therefore contingent.

C's remainder is subject to the condition that *B* not survive *A*. The condition is stated in the form of a condition precedent ("if [*B* does not survive *A*], to *C*") and, therefore, *C*'s remainder is contingent.

G retained a technical reversion. (There is always a reversion when a particular estate is followed by contingent remainders. In a case such as this example, the contingencies stated with respect to the interests of *B* and *C* exhaust all the possibilities; hence, the reversion is said to be merely "technical."[3]) The reversion is

---

[3]The presence of a technical reversion matters only in jurisdictions retaining the rule of the destructibility of contingent remainders, discussed in § 6.1.

vested subject to divestment because reversions are always vested rather than contingent.

The preceding examples—especially Examples 3.27 and 3.29—reveal that the distinction between a vested remainder subject to divestment and a contingent remainder rests on form, not substance. In both examples, *G* wants to subject *B*'s possession to the requirement that *B* outlive *A*. The only difference is the form of the requirement: a condition subsequent in Example 3.27 versus a condition precedent in Example 3.29. The distinction is artificial because the requirement can be stated either way. Yet the distinction is important to learn because substantive legal consequences can flow from the classification, as we shall see in Chapters 4-6.

A future interest that is subject to one or more limitations (recall the definition of this word: such interests expire naturally or by their own terms, e.g., an interest for life) is called *vested subject to limitational defeasance*. Only remainders and reversions can be vested subject to limitational defeasance.

Example 3.30: *G* transferred land "to *A* for life, then to *B* for life, then to *C*."

B's remainder is vested subject to limitational defeasance. It is sometimes referred to simply as a vested remainder for life. Note that *B* must survive *A* for his interest to become possessory. This implicit requirement of survival is not regarded as a "condition" of survival. Rather, *B*'s interest is regarded as terminating naturally upon his death, whether he dies before or after *A*'s death. In other words, *B*'s interest is a life estate just like *A*'s interest is a life estate, except that *B*'s life estate does not become possessory until *A* dies and therefore may never become possessory.

C's interest is a remainder because *B*'s interest is subject to a limitation and because it is an estate less than a fee simple. It is an indefeasibly vested remainder because it is subject to no condition or limitation.

Example 3.31: *G* conveyed land "to *A* for life, then to return to me for life, then to *C*."

This is the same as the previous example, except that the future interest subject to limitational defeasance is a reversion in *G* rather than a remainder in *B*.

Example 3.32: *G* transferred land "to *A* for life, then to *B* for 10 years, then to *C*."

B's remainder is vested subject to limitational defeasance. In this case, the time of *B*'s death is irrelevant. If *B* dies while *A* is still alive, *B*'s remainder will pass to her devisee or if she died intestate to her heirs. If *B* dies after *A*'s death but before the 10th anniversary thereof, the remaining portion of *B*'s 10-year term will pass to her devisee or if she died intestate to her heirs.

§ 3.8.3 Vested subject to open

Under the traditional system of classification, a future interest—typically a remainder—is *vested subject to open* when it is subject to no conditions precedent and when it is in favor of a class that contains at least one living member and that is still "open," i.e., where it is possible for additional persons to become class members (typically through birth or adoption). (On the concept of a class gift, see § 5.8.) Other and older labels for this type of interest are *vested subject to partial divestment* or *vested in quality but not in quantity*. These terms are descriptive of the phenomenon that each time a new member is added to the class the shares of the existing class members are reduced (partially divested). Whichever label is used, it is important to note that the existing class members are the ones who are regarded as having a remainder vested subject to open. The interests of the unborn or unadopted class members are contingent on being born or adopted. They are executory interests because upon birth or adoption they partially divest the interests or shares of the living class members.

> *Example 3.33: G* transferred land "to *A* for life, remainder to his children." When the transfer was made, *A* had two children, *X* and *Y*. Later a third child, *Z*, was born.
>
> At the time of the transfer, *X* has a vested remainder subject to open in an undivided half of the property; *Y* has a vested remainder subject to open in the other undivided half; the unborn children have executory interests. Upon *Z*'s birth, *Z*'s executory interest becomes a vested remainder subject to open in an undivided third of the property, and *X*'s and *Y*'s interests are reduced (or partially divested) to vested remainders subject to open in an undivided third.

The executory interest, the only other nonreversionary future interest, can be in favor of a class that is subject to open, but the executory interest itself cannot be called vested subject to open because executory interests are, almost by definition, contingent. (See footnote 5.)

§ 3.8.4 Contingent

Under the traditional system of classification, a future interest is *contingent* (nonvested)[4] if it is subject to a condition precedent. A condition precedent may be explicit or implicit. An explicit condition precedent exists where the language of the disposition declares that the interest is to become possessory *if* some event occurs. Implicit conditions precedent exist when the future interest is in favor of unborn or unascertained persons.

Remainders can be contingent but need not be. Executory interests are nearly always contingent.[5]

---

[4] The traditional term is *contingent*, but some authorities use the term *nonvested*.

[5] The typical executory interest is subject to a condition precedent and is classified as contingent. In rare cases, an executory interest is created that is unconditional. An example would be if *G* conveyed land "to *B* and his heirs, to take effect in possession 25 years from now." Another example would be if *G* conveyed land "to *B* and his heirs, to take effect in possession at my death." It is assumed in each case that the possessory interest retained by *G* is a fee simple interest, not a term of 25 years or a life estate. This means that *B*'s future interest cannot be a remainder and, therefore,

Reversions cannot be contingent but possibilities of reverter and rights of entry are regarded as contingent for most purposes (although not for the Rule Against Perpetuities).[6]

> *Example 3.34: G* conveyed land "to *A* for life, remainder to *B* if *B* survives *A*."
>
> *B*'s remainder is contingent because the condition of surviving *A* is stated in the form of a condition precedent—"to *B* if."
>
> *G*'s reversion appears to be subject to the condition precedent that *B* not survive *A*, but *G*'s reversion is vested subject to divestment

must be an executory interest. If it were a remainder, it would be classified as indefeasibly vested. The courts have been reluctant to call this type of an executory interest vested. Its classification has been perplexing because it is an executory interest. Nevertheless, it is generally assumed that, like vested interests in general, this type of an executory interest is not subject to the Rule Against Perpetuities.

[6]Although possibilities of reverter and rights of entry are classified as contingent, they are not subject to the Rule Against Perpetuities. This anomaly was noted by Professor John Chipman Gray in his classic treatise. Gray agreed that possibilities of reverter were, and should be, exempt from the Rule, and so he maintained that there was "no practical object" in labeling them as contingent. Gray on Perpetuities § 113.3. Conversely, Gray argued that rights of entry, as truly continent interests, should be subject to the Rule. *Id.* at § 310.

because of the rule that reversions are always vested. This means that *B*'s remainder in this situation acts like an executory interest because it potentially divests *G*'s reversion. Nevertheless, it is a remainder because its predominant feature is that it takes effect in possession, if at all, on the natural termination of *A*'s life estate.

Example 3.35: *G* transferred land "to *A* for life, remainder to *A*'s children." When the transfer was made, *A* had no children.

A's unborn children have contingent remainders. Their remainders, unlike *B*'s remainder in the previous example, are implicitly contingent on being born or adopted, but are not contingent on surviving *A*.

Example 3.36: *G* transferred land "to *A* for life, remainder to *A*'s heirs."

The remainder in favor of *A*'s heirs is contingent because it is in favor of unascertained persons. The persons who are *A*'s heirs cannot be ascertained until *A*'s death.

Nevertheless, any person who would be an heir of *A* if *A* were to die immediately is called an heir apparent or an heir expectant. The heirs expectant are regarded as having contingent remainders during *A*'s lifetime rather than mere expectancies. Thus it is sometimes said that they take by purchase rather than by succession or descent. Their remainders are implicitly contingent on their actually becoming *A*'s heirs when *A* dies.

Example 3.37: *G* transferred land "to *A* for life, remainder to *B*, but if *B* fails to survive *A*, to *C*."

The condition that *B* survive *A* is a condition subsequent as to *B*'s remainder ("to *B*, but if"), making it vested subject to divestment. *C*'s executory interest is contingent, for it is subject to the condition precedent that *B* not survive *A*.

Example 3.38: *(1)* *G* transferred land "to *A* and his heirs on condition that *A* never allow liquor to be sold on the premises, but if *A* allows liquor to be sold on the premises, the property is to go to *B*."

(2) *G* transferred land "to *A* and his heirs for as long as *A* never allows liquor to be sold on the premises, and upon *A*'s allowing liquor to be sold on the premises, the property is to go to *B*."

B's executory interest is subject to the condition that *A* allow liquor to be sold on the premises. In both Variations, the condition is in condition precedent form and, therefore, *B*'s executory interest is contingent.

Example 3.39: *(1)* *G* conveyed land "to *A* and his heirs on condition that *A* never allow liquor to be sold on the premises, but if *A* allows liquor to be sold on the premises, the grantor shall have the right to re-enter and take possession of the premises."

(2) *G* conveyed land "to *A* and his heirs for as long as *A* never allows liquor to be sold on the premises, and upon *A*'s allowing liquor to be sold on the premises, the premises are to revert to the grantor."

G's right of entry in Variation (1) and *G*'s possibility of reverter in Variation (2) would appear to be subject to the condition precedent that *A* allow liquor to be sold on the premises. Most authorities do in fact classify these interests as contingent.

§ 3.9 Future Interests in Sets Under the Traditional System: Rules of Thumb

Some rules of thumb can be helpful in mastering the traditional system of classification when future interests occur in sets. When a *defeasible fee simple* is followed by more than one nonreversionary future interest, only one of which can become possessory, all the future interests are executory interests, for a remainder cannot follow a fee simple estate. (Recall § 3.4.)

> *Example 3.40:* G transferred land "to *A* and his heirs, but if *A* allows liquor to be sold on the land, to *B* if *B* is then living, and if *B* is not then living, to *C*."
>
> *B* and *C* have executory interests.

When a *particular estate* (a life estate or term of years) is followed by more than one nonreversionary future interest, the first future interest will always be a remainder. The other or subsequent future interest(s), however, may be either remainders or executory interests. In determining which, the following rules apply:

☞ *Rule 1:* If the first future interest is a contingent remainder, the other nonreversionary future interests will also be contingent remainders.

☞ *Rule 2:* If the first future interest is a vested remainder subject to divestment, the other nonreversionary future interests will be executory interests.

The rules are illustrated in the following examples.

Example 3.41: G transferred land "to *A* for life, remainder to *B* if *B* survives *A*, but if not, to *C*."

Because *B* has a contingent remainder, *C* has a contingent remainder. For convenience, *B*'s and *C*'s interests are known as alternative contingent remainders.

Example 3.42: G transferred land "to *A* for life, remainder to *B*, but if *B* fails to survive *A*, to *C*."

Because *B*'s remainder is vested subject to divestment, *C* has an executory interest.

§ 3.10 Summary of Categories of Vesting Under the Traditional System

It may be helpful at this point to set forth the table (below) as a way of summarizing the categories of vesting—under the traditional system of classification—that are permissible for each of the five future interests at their inception.

PERMISSIBLE CATEGORIES	*FUTURE INTEREST OF VESTING AT INCEPTION*
Remainders	Indefeasibly Vested
	Vested Subject to Defeasance (Divestment or Limitation)
	Vested Subject to Open
	Contingent
Executory Interests	Contingent
Reversions	Indefeasibly Vested
	Vested Subject to Defeasance (Divestment or Limitation)
Possibilities of Reverter	Contingent
Rights of Entry	Contingent

§ 3.11 Permissible Changes in Classification Under the Traditional System Due to Subsequent Events

We learned in § 3.1 that reversionary interests do not become nonreversionary by virtue of a post-creation transfer to a transferee. Likewise, nonreversionary interests do not become reversionary by virtue of a post-creation transfer to the transferor.

Some changes in classification due to post-creation events are permissible, however. Specifically, executory interests can become remainders, contingent remainders can become vested remainders, and (unless the rule of the destructibility of contingent remainders applies, on which see § 6.1) remainders can become executory interests. Consider the following examples.

Example 3.43: G transferred land "to A for life, remainder to B, but if B fails to survive A, to C." B predeceases A.

At creation, B's interest is a vested remainder subject to divestment and C's interest is an executory interest.

At B's death, B's vested remainder is divested and C's executory interest becomes an indefeasibly vested remainder. This points to the misleading nature of a statement that is unfortunately often repeated by courts: that an executory interest cannot vest until it vests in possession. In fact, an executory interest can vest before becoming possessory by changing into a remainder.

Example 3.44: G transferred land "to A for life, remainder to B if B survives A, but if not, to C." B predeceases A.

At creation, B's and C's interests are alternative contingent remainders. At B's death, B's contingent remainder is defeated, G's technical reversion is divested, and C's contingent remainder becomes an indefeasibly vested remainder.

Example 3.45: G transferred land "to A for life, remainder to B if B lives to age 21." The destructibility rule has been abolished by statute in the jurisdiction.

If B reaches 21 while A is alive, B's contingent remainder becomes indefeasibly vested, and G's reversion is divested.

If B is younger than 21 when A dies, B's contingent remainder becomes an executory interest. G's reversion takes effect in possession upon *A*'s death as a fee simple subject to defeasance in favor of *B* if and when *B* later reaches 21.

Example 3.46: *G* transferred land "to *A* for life, remainder to *A*'s children, but if none of *A*'s children survives *A*, to *B*." When the transfer was made, *A* had no children. Later a child, *X*, was born to *A*. Thereafter, but still during *A*'s lifetime, *X* died. The destructibility rule has been abolished by statute in the jurisdiction.

At creation, *A*'s unborn children have contingent remainders, because they are subject to the implicit condition precedent of being born to or adopted by *A*. *B* has an alternative contingent remainder, and *G* has a technical reversion.

When *X* is born, *X* takes a vested remainder subject to divestment and subject to open. *B*'s interest and the interests of *A*'s unborn children change into executory interests, and *G*'s technical reversion is divested.

When *X* dies, *B*'s interests and the interests of *A*'s unborn children do not change back into alternative contingent remainders because *X* does not lose his interest. *X*'s interest, which remains subject to complete divestment only if *A* leaves *no* surviving children and to partial divestment if *A* has additional children, passes through *X*'s estate to *X*'s successors in interest.

§ 3.12 Future Interests Belonging to More Than One Category Under the Traditional System

Under the traditional system of classification, a future interest can be subject to open but the phrase "subject to open" will not appear in its classification because it is contingent. This does not mean that the interest is not actually subject to open; it merely means that the fact is not traditionally expressed.

Example 3.47: G transferred land "to *A* for life, remainder to *A*'s children who survive *A*; but if none survives *A*, to *B*."

The remainders in *A*'s children are contingent. They are also subject to open, but recognition of this fact by using the phrase "contingent subject to open" is not done.

§ 3.13 Vested and Contingent Future Interests Under the Restatement 3d of Property

The simplified system of classification in the

Restatement 3d of Property reduces the four categories of vesting to two: vested and contingent. A future interest is *vested* if it is certain to take effect in possession or enjoyment. A future interest is *contingent* if it might not take effect in possession or enjoyment.

Accordingly, future interests that, under the traditional system, were indefeasibly vested are now called "vested." Future interests that, under the traditional system, were vested subject to defeasance or contingent are now called "contingent."

The Restatement 3d of Property explains that a future interest that is "vested" or "contingent" can be *subject to open* if it is in favor of a class that is open to future entrants. See Restatement 3d of Property § 25.3 cmt. f.

§ 3.14 Summary of the Simplified System of the Restatement 3d of Property

The table below summarizes the simplified system of classification adopted by the Restatement 3d of Property.

PRESENT INTEREST	FUTURE INTEREST
Fee simple absolute	None
Fee simple defeasible	Reversion (Vested or Contingent)
	Remainder (Vested or Contingent)
Life estate	Reversion (Vested or Contingent)
	Remainder (Vested or Contingent)
Term of years	Reversion (Vested or Contingent)
	Remainder (Vested or Contingent)

§ 3.15 Does the Law Favor the Vesting of Estates?

The law of future interests traditionally preferred vested interests to contingent ones. As was colorfully stated in *Roberts v. Roberts*, 2 Bulstrode 123, 80 Eng. Rep. 1002 (K.B. 1613), "the law always delights in the vesting of estates, and contingencies are odious in the law, and are the causes of troubles, and vesting and settling of estates, the cause of repose and certainty."

The source of the preference for vested interests is complex, but it is commonly claimed that it arose from the desire to avoid certain common-law rules, such as the rule of the destructibility of contingent remainders (see § 6.1) and the Rule Against Perpetuities (see Chapter 5), to promote alienability, to promote completeness of the disposition, and to promote equality of distribution among different lines of descent.

The Restatement 3d of Property, having abolished the destructibility rule (see § 6.1) and having reformulated the system of classification (see above) and the Rule Against Perpetuities (see § 5.16), declines to endorse a preference for vested, as opposed to contingent, future interests. See Restatement 3d of Property §§ 11.3, 15.4 cmt. d, 25.3 cmt. d.

Perhaps the best way to describe the traditional preference for vested future interests is that the courts will construe a provision as not imposing a condition precedent if they can do so without contradicting the express language of the instrument, i.e., where there is sufficient ambiguity in the language to permit what might be called an even choice.

An illustration of this preference can be seen with respect to the remainder for life ("to *A* for life, then to *B* for life, then to *C*"). *B*'s remainder for life could in theory have been classified as contingent upon surviving *A*. In fact, remainders for life are held to become vested at the birth of the taker (here, *B*'s birth) and are vested subject to limitational defeasance (*B*'s eventual and certain death). This classification obtains even where survivorship is expressly phrased as a condition precedent, as in the following example.

Example 3.48: *G* transferred land "to *A* for life, remainder to *B* for life if *B* survives *A*."

Most courts ignore the express condition of survivorship as mere surplusage and classify *B*'s remainder as vested, not contingent.

Another illustration of the preference for vested interests can be seen with respect to remainders subject to a power of appointment. (We shall discuss powers in Part IV.) Frequently someone will be given a power to divert the property to someone other than the beneficiary of the remainder interest. This kind of condition is not considered a condition precedent.

Example 3.49: G transferred land "to A for life, remainder to the persons A shall by will appoint, and in default of appointment, to B."

B's remainder is vested subject to divestment by the exercise of the power by A.

A similar result is reached in cases involving a remainder subject to a charge or lien, as in the following example.

Example 3.50: G transferred land "to A for life, remainder B if B pays C $5,000 within in one year of A's death."

By the prevailing view, B takes the land at A's death subject to a charge or lien in favor of C. If B does not pay the $5,000 to C within a reasonable time, C can enforce the charge or lien in that amount against the land. Had the court instead held that B's remainder was contingent on paying the money, B would have lost the land and C would not have received the money; neither of these results accomplishes G's objective.

CHAPTER 4

TWO CONSEQUENCES OF THE CLASSIFICATION OF FUTURE INTERESTS

§ 4.1 Alienability
§ 4.2 Failure

In this chapter, we consider two consequences of the classification of future interests: (1) alienability and (2) failure. The classification may affect whether the future interest can be alienated. The classification may also affect what happens if the future interest fails.

§ 4.1 Alienability

The discussion of the alienability of future interests first must be divided into transfers at death (by will or by intestacy) and transfers during lifetime (inter vivos). After examining each of these voluntary transfers, we then consider the rights of creditors.

§ 4.1.1 Voluntary transfer at death: intestacy and will

Future interests are generally *descendible*, meaning capable of passing by intestacy. At one time, the course of descent for future interests was different from that of possessory estates. The details need not trouble us here; they are described in Simes & Smith on Future Interests § 1882; Am. L. Prop. § 4.73. The divergent course of descent for future interests was abolished by statute in England in 1897, and today in the United States reversions, remainders, and executory interests descend according to the same rules and in the same proportions as possessory estates. Everywhere except South Carolina, possibilities of reverter and rights of entry also descend according to the same rules applicable to possessory estates. In South Carolina, possibilities of reverter and rights of entry do not descend. See *Purvis v. McElveen*, 234 S.C. 94, 106 S.E.2d 913 (1959).

Future interests are also generally *devisable*, meaning capable of passing by will. This is true in all U.S. states for reversions, remainders, and executory interests, and in most states for possibilities of reverter and rights of entry. See Simes & Smith on Future Interests § 1903.

There is an obvious exception to the above rules, for interests conditioned upon the beneficiary's survival. A future interest is descendible and devisable only if the beneficiary's death does not extinguish the interest. Consider the following example.

Example 4.1: G transferred land "to A for life, remainder to B, but if B fails to survive A, to C." C died, then B, then A.

C's executory interest is not contingent on C's survival. Thus, C's executory interest is descendible and devisable.

B's remainder was vested subject to divestment if B failed to survive A. On these facts, B did die before A, hence the remainder was extinguished at B's death.

Under the Restatement 3d of Property, the devisability and descendability of a future interest do not depend upon classification. The position of the Restatment 3d of Property is stated in § 25.2 cmt. f: "All future interests are ... devisable and inheritable if the owner's death does not terminate the interest...."

§ 4.1.2 Voluntary transfer during life

Reversions and vested remainders have long been

alienable inter vivos. Contingent remainders were traditionally considered by the common law as inalienable inter vivos on the ground that they were too speculative; they were mere possibilities of receiving an interest in the future, rather than property interests in their own right. When executory interests were recognized, they were regarded as sufficiently analogous to contingent remainders to warrant the same treatment.

Despite this inalienability rule, holders of these contingent interests in England still found three ways to make transfers: contracts were enforceable if adequate consideration had been received by the transferor; deeds were enforceable if the deed contained a covenant of warranty, thereby estopping the transferor from challenging the transferee's title; and releases were enforceable if the release was in favor of the person whose future interest would be defeated if the released interest were to vest. Given these exceptions, the common-law rule of inalienability boiled down to this: purported transfers for inadequate consideration by quitclaim deed to someone other than a person in whose favor the interest could have been released were ineffective.

Today, most U.S. states have abolished the inalienability rule by statute or judicial decision, thus making contingent remainders and executory interests transferable inter vivos. A few states follow the common-law rule of inalienability while also recognizing the three forms of transfer that were available in England. A few other states make alienability depend upon the type of contingency: interests contingent on an event (surviving the life tenant, for example) are alienable, but interests contingent as to person (for instance, class gifts, in which some beneficiaries may be unborn or unascertained) are not.

Example 4.2: G transferred land "to *A* for life, remainder to *B* if *B* survives *A*; if not, to *B*'s heirs.*"*

B's remainder is contingent as to event, and under this rule would be alienable. The remainder in *B*'s heirs, however, is contingent as to person and would be inalienable.

But these are minority positions. Most U.S. states treat contingent remainders and executory interests as fully transferable.

There is an important sense, however, in which contingent interests are impossible to alienate, namely when there is no one who can consent to the alienation. Consider a transfer "to *A* for life, remainder to *A*'s children." If *A* has living children, their remainder interests can be alienated either by themselves if they possess legal capacity or, if not, by their legal guardian. But if *A* is childless, there may be no one—not even *A*—who can consent to the alienation. Guardians in the traditional sense can be appointed only for living persons. Many jurisdictions authorize a specially appointed fiduciary called a guardian ad litem to represent the interests of unborn or unascertained beneficiaries in litigation, but the law seldom authorizes this fiduciary to join in a transfer of property. For a statute authorizing such consent, see UTC § 305.

With respect to possibilities of reverter and rights of entry, U.S. jurisdictions are divided. Some permit alienation of one or both; others do not.

Under the Restatement 3d of Property, the alienability of a future interest does not depend upon its classification. The position of the Restatement 3d of Property is stated in § 25.2 cmt. f: "All future interests are alienable ... *unless the transferor has imposed a valid restraint on alienation.*"

The italicized qualification in the Restatement 3d of Property—"unless the transferor has imposed a valid restraint on alienation"—leads us to an important point: *no holder of a future interest may transfer the interest to the extent that the creator has imposed a valid restraint on alienation.* Today, most future interests are created in trusts, rather than directly in land (recall § 1.4), and the creator of the trust—known as the "settlor" of the trust—may impose a valid restraint, in the form of a *spendthrift clause*, on the beneficiary's power to alienate a present or future interest in the trust. A typical spendthrift clause provides: "No interest of any beneficiary in the income or principal of this trust shall be assignable in anticipation of payment or be liable in any way for the beneficiary's debts or obligations and shall not be subject to attachment." If a trust has a valid spendthrift clause, the trust is called a *spendthrift trust*. A beneficiary of a spendthrift trust is limited, and in many cases prevented, from transferring the beneficiary's interest to a third party. On the validity and effect of spendthrift clauses, see generally Restatement 3d of Trusts ch. 12.[1]

---

[1] On the validity and effect of restraints on the alienation of future interests created directly in land, see generally Restatement 2d of Property ch. 4.

§ 4.1.3 Involuntary transfer: creditors' rights

State statutes provide creditors with the right to impound their debtors' assets prior to judgment and the right after judgment to subject their assets to sale.[2] These statutes purport to specify the types

---

[2]There is a potential problem with selling future interests to satisfy creditors: the sale of a future interest that is subject to conditions will undoubtedly bring a low purchase price. In such an event, the sale would not substantially benefit the creditor and might do serious harm to the debtor by depriving him or her of the future possibility of gaining property of much higher value. The winner in such situations is neither the debtor nor the creditor but the purchaser at the sale. (There is, of course, the chance that the purchaser may be the creditor.) In a tiny handful of cases, courts have responded to this problematic scenario by exercising their equitable powers to depart from the general rule on creditors' rights in cases involving equitable future interests, meaning future interests in trust. In at least one case, the court held that the future interest was subject to contingencies so remote that the creditor should simply be denied access to it. *Clarke v. Fay*, 205 Mass. 228, 91 N.E. 328 (1910). In another case, the court permitted access but refused to order an immediate sale of the interest, imposing instead a lien on the future interest until the contingencies were satisfied, if ever. *Meyer v. Reif*, 217 Wis. 11, 258 N.W. 391(1935). We find this last solution—a lien—a promising alternative to the immediate sale. It is worth considering for all equitable future interests, even ones

of assets that are subject to these procedures, but the statutory language is usually so general that courts must decide whether the debtor's future interests can be affected.

The general principle followed by the courts under these statutes is that if the future interest is voluntarily alienable, it is also subject to the claims of creditors. Indefeasibly vested remainders and reversions are voluntarily alienable, hence available to creditors. The same is true of remainders and reversions that are vested subject to defeasance.

Contingent remainders and executory interests are not subject to the claims of creditors in the minority of states in which they are not voluntarily alienable. The fact that the English methods of conveyance (the equitable contract to convey, the estoppel by deed, and the release) are available does not change the result. In the vast majority of states, these interests can be alienated, and the

---

not subject to remote contingencies. No future interest, even one indefeasibly vested, would bring a sale price equal to the value of immediate possession of the trust fund, hence the attractiveness of a lien rather than an immediate judgment sale.

courts rather routinely hold such interests subject to creditors' claims. See Restatement of Property §§ 166, 167.

To re-state the general rule: if the future interest is voluntarily alienable, it is subject to the claims of creditors. But recall from the previous section (§ 4.1.2) that a future interest is not voluntarily alienable if the creator has imposed a valid restraint on alienation. As we observed, such a restraint typically takes the form of a spendthrift clause in a trust instrument. This raises an important question: to what extent can the creditor of a trust beneficiary reach the beneficiary's interest if the trust has a valid spendthrift clause? In most instances, the creditor must wait until the trustee makes a distribution of trust property (income or principal) to the beneficiary.[3] However, some creditors—for example, the beneficiary's spouse, former spouse, and children seeking support or alimony—have

---

[3] The extent to which a creditor can compel the trustee to make a distribution is a matter of debate. Compare Restatement 3d of Trusts § 60 (permitting creditors to compel a distribution if the beneficiary could compel a distribution) with Uniform Trust Code § 504(b) (providing that a creditor cannot compel a distribution even if the beneficiary could do so).

preferred status and can reach the beneficiary's interest. See Restatement 3d of Trusts § 59.

So far we have been speaking of a creditor's rights under state law during the debtor's lifetime. This leaves two topics to be addressed. First, the creditor's rights under state law after the debtor's death. Second, a creditor's rights under federal bankruptcy law.

When the owner of a future interest dies, the interest might be transmissible by will even if it was not alienable inter vivos. It may be argued that the decedent's creditors should be satisfied from such assets. There appears to be little law on the subject. Some state statutes governing the payment of claims against decedents' estates answer the matter by equating the creditor's rights to the property that the decedent could have alienated inter vivos. Text writers and the Restatement of Property § 169 indicate that the same result will probably be reached in situations where the controlling statute is not explicit.

In federal bankruptcy proceedings, the rights of creditors are far-reaching. Federal law treats "all legal or equitable [property] interests of the debtor" as part of the bankrupt's estate "notwithstanding any provision in ... nonbankruptcy law ... that restricts ... transfer of such interest by the debtor ...." 11 U.S.C. § 541. This language is broad enough to include all classifications of future interests, even those immune from creditors under state law.

§ 4.2 Failure

A nonreversionary future interest can fail for any variety of reasons. The beneficiary might predecease the testator or predecease a subsequent time to which survival is required by the terms of the disposition; the future interest might be disclaimed; it might violate the Rule Against Perpetuities (on which see Chapter 5); and so on.

In general, a future interest that fails, regardless of the reason, is treated as if it had not been created. A particular problem exists, however, if the failed future interest is an executory interest following a fee simple estate. On this point, courts have reached different results depending on whether the estate is a fee simple determinable or a fee simple subject to a condition subsequent. Consider the following examples.

Example 4.3: G transferred land "to X Church so long as the land is used for church purposes, and if church use ever ceases, to B."

X Church has a fee simple determinable, and *B* has an executory interest.

Example 4.4: G transferred land "to X Church on condition that the land is used for church purposes, and if church use ever ceases, to *B*." X Church has a fee simple subject to a condition subsequent, and *B* has an executory interest.

In each of these two examples, *B*'s executory interest violates the Rule Against Perpetuities and is therefore invalid. The question is: what is the effect of the invalidity? According to the case law, the church's interest in Example 4.3 remains a fee simple determinable with a possibility of reverter in *G*, whereas the church's interest in Example 4.4 becomes a fee simple absolute. *First Universalist Soc'y of North Adams v. Boland*, 155 Mass. 171, 29 N.E. 524 (1892); *Proprietors of the Church in Brattle Square v. Grant*, 69 Mass. 142 (1855). A different view appears in the Restatement 2d of Property § 1.5 cmts. b & c, which suggest that the church's interest in both instances should be a fee simple absolute. The Restatement 3d of Property facilitates this result by eliminating the subcategories within the estate in fee simple defeasible (see § 2.4 above).

CHAPTER 5

THE RULE AGAINST PERPETUITIES

§ 5.1 Introduction

The Rule Against Perpetuities was originally designed to prevent the dead hand from indirectly curtailing the alienability of property for too long a period—in perpetuity. The indirect curtailment of alienability was said to arise from attaching contingencies to future interests in property.

A rule that developed, step by step over time, into the rule known today as the Rule Against Perpetuities was initiated in the much-celebrated *Duke of Norfolk's Case*, 3 Ch. Cas. 1, 22 Eng. Rep. 931 (Ch. 1682). The so-called modern Rule Against Perpetuities was formulated by Professor John Chipman Gray in the second edition of his book, The Rule Against Perpetuities (2d ed. 1906). Professor Gray's book solidified the Rule Against Perpetuities, stunting its further evolution throughout much of the twentieth century. But the Rule Against Perpetuities is again undergoing change. We analyze these changes toward the end of this chapter.

§ 5.2 Statement of the Rule at Common Law

The classic statement of the Rule Against Perpetuities was formulated by Professor John Chipman Gray in the second edition of his book,

The Rule Against Perpetuities (2d ed. 1906):

> *No [contingent future] interest is good unless it must vest, if at all, not later than 21 years after some life in being at the creation of the interest.*

Nothing resembling this mechanically precise "rule" was stated by the judge in the *Duke of Norfolk's Case*, the Lord Chancellor, the First Earl of Nottingham. His pronouncements about prohibiting perpetuities appear to be mere musings:

> But what Time? And where are the Bounds of that Contingency? You may limit, it seems, upon a Contingency to happen in a Life: What if it be limited, if such a one die without Issue within twenty-one Years, or 100 Years, or while Westminster-Hall stands? Where will you stop, if you do not stop here? I will tell you where I will stop: I will stop wherever any visible Inconvenience doth appear;....

Gradually, over the 150 or so years following the *Duke of Norfolk's Case*, the pronouncement that a contingency limited to "happen in a Life" was valid, but beyond that, an invalidity would arise "wherever any visible Inconvenience doth appear," grew step by step into the Rule Against Perpetuities stated by Professor Gray.

§ 5.3 Interests Subject to the Rule at Common Law

At common law, the Rule Against Perpetuities applies to future interests in property, whether legal or equitable, but only if they are contingent (nonvested). Classification of the interests in a disposition is, therefore, a preliminary but crucial step to solving perpetuity questions. Specifically, the Rule applies to contingent remainders and to executory interests, both of which are contingent future interests. The Rule does not apply to vested remainders, not even to those that are vested subject to defeasance; nor does the Rule apply to reversions, which are always vested. The other two reversionary future interests—possibilities of reverter and rights of entry—are also considered exempt from the Rule Against Perpetuities.[1]

---

[1]See § 3.8.4 note 6. Some states have statutes that terminate possibilities of reverter and rights of entry after a certain time. The statutes vary, but they generally state that these interests terminate if the event upon which they are predicated has not occurred within a fixed period (e.g., 30 years). The effect of the termination is to render the possessory estate absolute.

Class gifts (such as a transfer to "children" or "descendants"; see § 5.8) are also subject to the Rule, and in fact are treated specially. The early English decision of *Leake v. Robinson*, 2 Mer. 363, 35 Eng. Rep. 979 (Ch. 1817), laid down the proposition that *if the interest of any potential class member might vest too remotely, the entire class gift is invalid.* This is the so-called all-or-nothing rule, by which it is meant that a class gift is either completely valid or completely invalid. It is not permissible to treat the interest of each class member separately and say that some class members have valid interests and other class members have invalid interests.

§ 5.4   The "Perpetuity Period" at Common Law

The common-law perpetuity period is defined as a life in being plus 21 years. The period can be extended by one or more periods of gestation, *but only when an actual pregnancy makes the extension necessary.*

The life in being, often called the *measuring life*, must be the life of a person "in being at the creation of the interest." This means that the person whose life is the measuring life must be alive or in gestation when the perpetuity period begins to run.

The measuring life must also be a human life—the life of a corporation, an animal, or a plant cannot be used. But there are no further restrictions. Theoretically, anyone in the world who was alive or in gestation when the interest was created can be the measuring life. As a practical matter, though, it is not that complex, as we shall see, when one gets down to identifying the measuring life in actual cases.

As noted above, a child in gestation at the commencement of the perpetuity period can be a measuring life because the child is considered then to be "in being." So also the perpetuity period is expandable at the end to account for an actual period of gestation, if necessary.

§ 5.5   The Requirement of Initial Certainty

Implicit in Professor Gray's formulation is the *requirement of initial certainty*, which is that a contingent future interest is invalid if, at the creation of the interest, there exists any possible chain of events that might subsequently arise that would allow the interest to remain contingent beyond a life in being plus 21 years. The life in being is traditionally called the "measuring life."

Only valid dispositions produce a particular life who has the requisite causal connection and is identified as the so-called measuring life. An invalid interest is invalid because there is *no* measuring life that makes it valid—not because it might remain contingent beyond 21 years after the death of an identifiable measuring life. This is what is meant when it is said that invalidity under the common-law Rule depends upon the existence, as of the interest's creation, of an invalidating chain of possible post-creation events. *The search for a "measuring life," therefore, turns out in reality to be a search for a "validating life."*

The requirement of initial certainty is a mechanism for testing the validity of an interest *in advance* of its actual vesting or termination. With the decision made in advance, the common law has no need to mark off a "perpetuity period" in the case of invalid interests. Here is why: A "perpetuity period" would be necessary only if actual post-creation events were to be taken into account. But the common-law Rule does not permit post-creation events to be considered.

§ 5.6 How to Search for a Validating Life

The Official Comment to § 1 of the Uniform Rule sets forth the following guidance for solving a perpetuities problem:

> The process for determining whether a validating life exists is to postulate the death of each individual connected in some way to the transaction, and ask the question: Is there with respect to this individual an invalidating chain of possible [post-creation] events? If one individual can be found for whom the answer is No, that individual can serve as the validating life. As to that individual there will be the requisite causal connection between his or her death and the questioned interest's vesting or terminating no later than 21 years thereafter.

Note that the converse is also true: If no such person can be found, there is no validating life; an interest for which there is no validating life is invalid.

In searching for a validating life, there is no formal rule forbidding the testing of anyone in the world to see if that person has the causal connection demanded by the requirement of initial certainty. There is, for example, no law against testing your favorite movie star or rock star in each case, if you want to do that. But experience has shown that no outsider will pass the test.

What we mean to say is that you can safely limit the persons you test to insiders—those who are connected in some way to the transaction. Only insiders have a chance of supplying the requisite causal connection demanded by the requirement of initial certainty. The insiders to be tested vary from situation to situation, but would always include: the transferor; the beneficiaries of the disposition, including but not restricted to the taker or takers of the challenged interest; the powerholder and permissible appointees of a power of appointment; persons related to the foregoing by blood or adoption; and anyone else who has any connection to the transaction. If there is any doubt about a particular person, no harm is done by subjecting that person to the test. Usually it takes no more than an instant to resolve whether or not a person arguably on the fringe of the transaction has the requisite causal connection demanded by the requirement of initial certainty.

There is, however, no point in even considering the life of a complete outsider who is clearly unconnected to the transaction—a person selected at random from the world at large—just because the outsider happened to be in being at the creation of the interest. Outsiders in that category have already been tested and found *always* to be wanting. No outsider can possibly fulfill the requirement of initial certainty because there will always be an invalidating chain of possible post-creation events as to every outsider who might be proposed: any outsider can immediately die after the creation of the interest without having any effect on when the interest will vest or terminate.

Example 5.1: G devised land "to my son *A* for life, remainder to *A*'s children who live to age 21."

The interest in question is the contingent remainder in *A*'s children. To determine whether that interest is valid, you must test the insiders in this transaction to see if any of them satisfies the requirement of initial certainty. If yes, that person is the validating life. The obvious candidate to test is *A*. *A* satisfies the requirement of initial certainty here, because none of *A*'s children can reach age 21 (or die under age 21) beyond 21 years after *A*'s death.

Example 5.2: G devised land "to my daughter B for life, remainder to A's children who live to age 21."

The obvious insiders to test first in this case are A and B. Although B is the life tenant, she does not satisfy the requirement of initial certainty. A chain of possible post-creation events that disqualifies her is that A might have a child who reaches age 21 (or dies under age 21) more than 21 years after her death. A does satisfy the requirement of initial certainty, as we saw in the previous example. This remains true here, even though he is not a devisee.

In appropriate cases, the validating life need not be individuated. Rather, the life can be a member of a group of individuals. It is common in these cases to say that the members of the group are the validating *lives*. This is acceptable, as long as it is recognized that the true meaning of the statement is that the validating *life* is the life of the member of the group who turns out to live the longest. As was said in *Skatterwood v. Edge*, 1 Salk. 229, 91 Eng. Rep. 203 (K.B. 1697), "for let the lives be never so many, there must be a survivor, and so it is but the length of that life; for [Justice] Twisden used to say, the candles were all lighted at once."

Example 5.3: G devised land "to my grandchildren who live to age 21."

The grandchildren's springing executory interest does not violate the common-law Rule. The validating life is the longest to live of *G*'s children. It is impossible for any of *G*'s grandchildren to reach age 21—or die under age 21—more than 21 years after the death of *G*'s last surviving child.

A well established but sometimes overlooked point is that the recipient of an interest might himself be the validating life. This point is especially useful where an interest is contingent on the recipient's reaching an age in excess of 21 or is contingent on the recipient's survival of a particular point in time that is or may be in excess of 21 years after the interest was created or after the death of a person in being at the date of creation.

Example 5.4: G devised land "to my son *A*'s children who are living 25 years after my death." *A* predeceased *G*. At *G*'s death, *A* had three living children.

The executory interest created in *A*'s children does not violate the common-law Rule. *A*'s children are their own validating lives. Each child will either survive the 25-year period or fail to do so within his or her own lifetime. To say this another way, we will know no later than at the death of each child whether or not that child survived the required period.

Dispositions of property sometimes create more than one interest that is subject to the Rule. When this happens, you must test the validity of each interest separately. A life that validates one interest might or might not validate the other interests. Consequently, you must search for a validating life for each interest.

§ 5.7 Time of Creation

The time when a property interest is created is important because it fixes the time when the validating life must be "in being." It is also important because it demarks the facts that can be taken into account in determining the validity of an interest. Under the common-law Rule, an interest is valid only if, at the time when the interest is created, with the facts *then existing* taken into account, the interest is certain to vest or terminate within a life in being plus 21 years. The facts that actually occur from that time forward are irrelevant; all that counts is what *might* happen.

Property interests created by will are created when the testator dies, not when the testator signs the will. Thus the validating life for testamentary transfers must be a person who was alive (or in gestation) when the testator died, and the facts that can be taken into account in determining the validity of an interest created by will are those existing at the testator's death.

Property interests created by inter vivos transfers are created when the transfers become effective for purposes of property law generally. In most cases, this occurs when the deed conveying the property is delivered to the transferee(s), for this is the point at which the transfer becomes irrevocable. Consistent with this principle, property interests in revocable inter vivos trusts are considered created for perpetuity purposes when the power to revoke expires, typically at the death of the settlor of the trust.

§ 5.8   Class Gifts

A class gift is a gift to persons who are described by a group label, such as "children" or "descendants," and who are intended to take as a group. A typical feature of a class gift is that the membership of the group is able to increase or decrease, meaning that persons can be added or dropped as events (such as births, adoptions, or deaths) unfold in the future.

A gift is likely a class gift if the group members are *only* identified by a group label (such as "my children"). See Restatement 3d of Property § 13.1 cmt. g.

A gift is likely *not* a class gift, despite a group label, if the takers are also identified by name (such as "my children, *A*, *B*, and *C*"). Instead, this disposition is typically considered as a series of separate gifts of a fractional share of the property. See Restatement 3d of Property § 13.2 cmt. c.

The law treats these as presumptions that can be rebutted if "the language or circumstances indicate that the transferor intended" a contrary result. Restatement 3d of Property § 13.1(b), 13.2(c). But the case law shows that the presumptions are seldom rebutted in practice. Accordingly, the examples in this *Nutshell* assume that the presumptions have not been rebutted.

A typical feature of a class gift is the ability of the group to fluctuate in number. This occurs through an *increase* in the number of takers (by births or adoptions) or through a *decrease* in the number of takers (by deaths).

The ability to fluctuate in number does not continue forever. Births, adoptions, or deaths can cause fluctuations only if they occur within a finite period of time. As a general proposition, once the time of possession has arrived, fluctuation comes to an end. However, as we shall see, this is only a general proposition, and the time limit on increase and the time limit on decrease are not always identical. That is, the ability of a given class gift to increase might expire before its ability to decrease, and vice versa. The point is that each time limit must be analyzed separately. Identifying these time limits is a crucial preliminary step toward determining the validity of the class gift under the Rule Against Perpetuities, for as we shall see, a class gift violates the common-law Rule if the gift is subject to increase or decrease beyond a life in being plus 21 years.

A class gift is *subject to decrease* if the gift is subject to a requirement of survival. A class member who fails to fulfill a requirement of survival drops out of the class. But there is an additional consequence: his or her lost share is added to the shares of the other members of the class who do become entitled to participate. This feature is intrinsic to class gifts—the built-in or implicit *gift over* to the other members of the class.

In the case of *testamentary* transfers, only devisees who survive the testator are entitled to take. This implicit requirement of survival is imposed by the common law, and applies to class gifts and individual gifts alike. The difference between class gifts and individual gifts arises from the fact that there is no built-in gift over to the other takers in the case of individual gifts. Consider the following example.

Example 5.5: G devised land "to my children in equal shares." When the will was executed, *G* had three children (*A*, *B*, and *C*). *A* predeceased *G*. *B* and *C* survived *G*.

Because *G*'s will created a class gift, *B* and *C* each take an undivided one-half interest in the devised land.

If *G*'s will had created individual gifts ("to my three children, *A*, *B*, and *C*"), *A*'s lost one-third share would not have been added to the shares of *B* and *C*; it would have passed to *G*'s residuary devisees or, in the absence of an effective residuary clause, to *G*'s heirs.

Because a class gift such as the one in the preceding example is an immediate testamentary gift in fee simple absolute, it is subject to decrease between the time of the execution of the will and the time of the testator's death. Once the testator has died, the ability to decrease comes to an end. Thus, if after G's death B dies survived by C, B's one-half interest would not be divested in favor of C.

Suppose, however, that the class gift is a *future* interest rather than an immediate one in fee simple absolute. Here the question of whether the ability to decrease continues beyond the testator's death depends on whether a condition of survival is attached to the class gift.

Example 5.6: G devised land "to my daughter A for life, remainder to A's children." G was survived by A and by A's three children (X, Y, and Z). Z died during A's lifetime. X and Y survived A.

The class (consisting of X, Y, and Z as of G's death) is not allowed to decrease beyond G's death. The reason is that no express condition of survival was attached to the children's remainder interest.[2] Consequently, upon A's

_____

[2]This analysis is based on the common-law rule that a future interest is not subject to a condition of survival of the life tenant unless one is expressly imposed. This rule may be changed by statute. UPC § 2-707, for example, presumptively

death, X, Y, and Z (i.e., Z's successor in interest) each take an undivided one-third share in the devised land. Z does not drop out of the class because of her death between the deaths of G and A.

If G's will had expressly imposed a condition of survival ("to my daughter A for life, remainder to A's children who survive A"), then the class would have continued to be subject to decrease beyond G's death. On these facts, Z would have dropped out of the class. Z's lost one-third share would have been added to the shares of X and Y. Upon A's death, X and Y would each receive an undivided one-half share in the devised land.[3]

makes all future interests *in trust* subject to a condition precedent of survival and provides that the deceased person's surviving descendants take the share that the deceased person would have taken had he or she survived; thus, had G's devise been in trust, Z's one-third share would be divided among Z's descendants who survived A, and would go to X and Y only if Z left no such descendants.

[3] This analysis is based on the common law. Had G's devise been in trust, UPC § 2-707 provides that Z's one-third share would be divided among Z's descendants who survived A, and would go to X and Y only if Z left no such descendants.

Thus far, we have been discussing a decrease in the number of takers of a class gift. The number of takers is also able to *increase*. The following example develops the difference between class gifts and individual gifts on this point.

Example 5.7: G devised land "to my children." When the will was executed, *G* had two children, *A* and *B*. Later *G* had a third child, *C. G* was survived by all three children.

Because *G*'s will created a class gift, *A*, *B*, and *C* each take an undivided one-third share in the devised land.

If *G*'s will had created individual gifts ("to my children, *A* and *B*"), the result would have been different. The shares of *A* and *B* would have remained constant at one-half each.[4]

---

[4]This analysis is based on the common law. UPC § 2-302 provides that *C* would take an equal share in the devised land unless it is proved that *G* intentionally excluded *C*. Statutes in nearly all non-UPC states provide that *C* would take an intestate share unless it is proved that *G* intentionally excluded *C*; *C*'s intestate share would ordinarily be paid out of *G*'s residuary estate rather than out of the devised land.

A class is subject to increase—subject to open—as long as new entrants can come into the class. The ability of a class to increase ends—the class "closes"—at the *earlier* of two events: (1) the natural (or physiological) closing of the class;[5] or (2) the artificial (or premature) closing brought about by the application of the rule of convenience.

The natural closing of a class occurs when births (or, if adopted members are within the class description, adoptions) become physiologically impossible. A class gift in favor of a transferor's grandchildren physiologically closes upon the death of the transferor's last living child. A grandchild who is in gestation on the date the class

[5]Under traditional property law, death is deemed to terminate the possibility of having children. New technologies, however, make it possible in practice to have children by assisted reproduction after death. The Restatement 3d of Property § 15.1 cmt. j adopts a new rule that such children "be treated as in being at the decedent's death, for purposes of the class-closing rules, if the child was born within a reasonable time after the decedent's death." See also Uniform Probate Code § 2-120(k), which provides that a posthumously conceived child is treated as in gestation at an individual's death "if the child is: (1) in utero not later than 36 months after the individual's death; or (2) born not later than 45 months after the individual's death."

closes is regarded as in being on the closing date.

A class may close earlier than its physiological closing. When this happens, the class has been closed artificially. Artificial closing is governed by the *rule of convenience*.

The rule of convenience is a rule of construction, not a rule of law. It yields to a contrary intent. In practice, however, a contrary intent can seldom be shown, and consequently the rule of convenience typically prevails.

Once a class has been closed by the rule of convenience, subsequently conceived or adopted persons are not entitled to participate in the class gift, even though they otherwise fit the class label. New entrants come into a class only if they are conceived[6] or adopted[7] while the class is still open.

The rule of convenience holds that a class closes when a class member becomes entitled to distribution of a share. This rule is founded on two

[6]A child in gestation when a class closes is regarded as in being at that time. To enter the class, the child must be born alive and probably must be born viable.

[7]With respect to an adopted child, the date of adoption, not the date of conception, is the significant date.

basic premises. First is the premise that the use of only a group or class description indicates that all persons who fit the description, whenever born or adopted, were intended to share in the gift. In other words, the starting point is that the class was not intended to close until it closes naturally. Second, because of inherent difficulties or "inconveniences" in allowing participation by persons born or adopted after distribution, it is believed that the transferor, if the transferor had contemplated the difficulties, would have intended to exclude these persons. That is, although the basic intent of the transferor is to keep the class open until it closes naturally, if inconveniences will arise from doing so, the transferor would prefer for the class to be closed prematurely, so that the inconveniences will be avoided.

The inconvenience of a class being kept open after distribution is that the distributees would not take an indefeasible interest. Instead, they would receive a considerably less useful defeasible one. Taking an interest that is subject to being partially divested upon the birth or adoption of additional class members would render the property less marketable and, if personal property, would require some device such as the posting of security to protect the interests of unborn or unadopted members of the class.

Example 5.8: G devised land "to my grandchildren." When G executed her will, her only child, *A*, had a child, *X*. Later, but before *G*'s death, *A* had a second child, *Y*. G then died, survived by *A*, *X*, and *Y*.

Under the rule of convenience, the class remains open until *G*'s death but closes when G died even though *A* is alive and therefore is deemed capable of having more children. *X* and *Y* each take an undivided estate in one half of the devised land in fee simple absolute. In other words, their estates are not subject to partial divestment in favor of any later-born or later-adopted children of *A*.

The rule of convenience does not operate if there is no class member entitled to distribution.

Example 5.9: G devised land "to my grandchildren." At *G*'s death, *G*'s only child *A* was alive but had no children.

The rule of convenience does not close the class at *G*'s death. Rather, the class remains open until it closes naturally, at *A*'s death. The only feasible alternative would be to nullify the class gift entirely. It is thought that few testators would desire this result.

The same principles apply to class gifts in which possession is postponed—i.e., to future interests created in a class. Consider the following example.

Example 5.10: G devised land "to my daughter A for life, remainder to my son B's children." G was survived by A, B, and B's child, X. B later had a second child, Y, during A's lifetime, and a third child, Z, after A's death.

The class continues to be subject to increase beyond G's death and during A's lifetime. It closes on A's death even though B is still alive and is deemed capable of having more children. X and Y will clearly be able to participate. Z will be entitled to participate only if Z was in gestation at A's death.

Suppose instead that by the time of A's death no children had been born to B and that none was then in gestation. This situation is treated consistently with Example 5.9. The class would not close at A's death but rather would remain open until it closes physiologically—at B's death.[8]

---

[8]This assumes that the destructibility rule (see § 6.1) has been abolished in the jurisdiction.

We can now turn to the application of the Rule Against Perpetuities to class gifts. The governing principle is the all-or-nothing rule, which we encountered earlier in § 5.3. That rule states: *If the interest of any potential class member might vest too remotely, the entire class gift is invalid.* In other words, a class gift is either completely valid or completely invalid. It is not permissible to treat the interest of each class member separately and say that some class members have valid interests and other class members have invalid interests. See Restatement of Property §§ 371, 383, 384.

Example 5.11: G devised land "to my son *A* for life, then to *A*'s children who live to age 25." *G* was survived by *A* and by *A*'s two children, *X* and *Y*. *X* had reached 25 at *G*'s death, but *Y* was under 25.

The class gift in *A*'s children who reach 25 is invalid. *X* and *Y* are their own validating lives, but there is no validating life for children born to or adopted by *A* after *G*'s death. Note that the rule of convenience does not close the class at *G*'s death, because the time of distribution for *A*'s children is *A*'s death, not *G*'s death.

Two types of class gifts are exempt from the all-or-nothing rule: specific-sum class gifts and gifts to sub-classes. These special types of class gifts are exempt because the rationale of the all-or-nothing rule does not apply to them. Accordingly, each interest can be judged separately; the invalidity of one interest does not affect the validity of another.

Specific-sum class gifts give a specific amount of money to each class member, for example "$10,000 to each of my grandchildren who reach 25." This is different from the conventional class gift, wherein a sum of money or item of property is to be divided proportionally among the class members.

Gifts to sub-classes involve the subdivision of a class gift into separate shares, for example "to each of my daughter *A*'s children for their respective lives, and on the death of each child the proportionate share of corpus of the one so dying shall go to the children of such child."

In each case, the rationale of the all-or-nothing rule does not apply, because the transferor has divided the gift such that the interest of one class member (or sub-class) does not impinge on another.

§ 5.9   Constructional Preference for Validity

Professor Gray stated that a will or deed is to be construed without regard to the Rule Against Perpetuities, and then the Rule is to be applied "remorselessly" to the provisions so construed. Gray on Perpetuities § 629. Some courts may still adhere to this proposition. Most courts, we believe, would now be inclined to adopt the proposition put forward by the Restatement of Property § 375, which is that where an instrument is ambiguous—that is, where it is fairly susceptible to two or more constructions, one of which causes a Rule violation and the other of which does not—the construction that does not result in a Rule violation should be adopted.

One manifestation of the constructional preference for validity is the *principle of separability*, which courts invoke when an interest is subject to alternative contingencies, one of which causes a Rule violation. Suppose, for example, that property is devised "to *B* if X-event or Y-event happens." If there is no validating life for X-event but there is one for Y-event, courts will typically strike the invalid contingency so that the devise is altered to read "to *B* if Y-event happens." Consider the following example.

Example 5.12: G devised the residue of his estate "to my daughter *A* for life, then to *A*'s children who survive *A* and live to age 25, but if none of *A*'s children survives *A* or if none of *A*'s children who survives *A* lives to age 25, then to *B*." *G* was survived by *A*.

The class gift in *A*'s children is invalid and is replaced by a reversion in *G*'s heirs.

What about *B*'s executory interest? The separability principle divides it into two interests: one contingent on none of *A*'s children surviving *A*, and the other contingent on none of *A*'s children who survives *A* living to age 25. The first of these, but not the second, is valid. Consequently, the language "or if none of *A*'s children who survives *A* lives to age 25" is in effect stricken from the devise. *B* takes if none of *A*'s children survives *A*.

Because the separability principle saves one of *B*'s executory interests, the reversion in *G*'s heirs is vested subject to divestment in favor of *B* if none of *A*'s children survives *A*.

Note that the principle of separability is applicable only when the transferor has *expressly* stated the contingencies in the alternative. Where alternative contingencies are merely implicit, no separation will be recognized. In the words of Sir George

Jessel, Master of the Rolls, in *Miles v. Harford*, 12 Ch.D. 691 (Ch. 1879), "that is what [the courts] mean by splitting, they will not split the expression by dividing the two events, but when they find two expressions they give effect to both of them as if you had struck the other out of the will." Consider the following example.

Example 5.13: G devised the residue of his estate "to my son *A* for life, then to *A*'s children who survive *A* and live to age 25, but if none of *A*'s children does so, then to *B*." *A* survived *G*.

The class gift in *A*'s children is invalid and is replaced by a reversion in *G*'s heirs.

What about *B*'s executory interest? The separability principle cannot apply, because *B*'s interest is subject to one condition precedent, not two, namely the condition that "none of *A*'s children does so." Accordingly *B*'s interest is completely invalid, and the reversion in *G*'s heirs is indefeasibly vested.

§ 5.10   Consequences of Invalidity

When an interest is invalid because it violates the common-law Rule Against Perpetuities, the invalid interest is stricken from the disposition. Unless the doctrine of infectious invalidity (see below) applies, the other interests created by the disposition (assuming that none of them violates the Rule) take effect as if the invalid interest had never been created.

Example 5.14: G devised real property "to my son A for life, then to A's children for the life of the survivor, and upon the death of A's last surviving child, to A's grandchildren." G devised her residuary estate to her husband, H. G was survived by A and H.

Due to the invalidity of the remainder to A's grandchildren, the disposition reads as if that remainder interest had never been created: "to my son A for life, then to A's children for the life of the survivor." Since G's devise did not validly dispose of all interests in the parcel of real property, the undisposed-of interest passes under G's residuary clause to H. This testamentary transfer of the remainder interest to H is deemed to have occurred at G's death. Thus when A's last surviving child dies, the property goes to H (or H's successor in interest).

Note that if G's original devise had been in her residuary clause, the undisposed-of interest would have been intestate property and would have passed at G's death to her heirs.

Example 5.15: G devised land "to my daughter *A* for life, then for life to such of *A*'s children as reach 25, then to *B*." *G* was survived by *A* and *B*.

The remainder for life to *A*'s children is invalid. The effect of striking it is not to create a gap that must be filled by the residuary clause. Rather it is to accelerate *B*'s remainder; the devise now reads "to *A* for life, then to *B*."

In appropriate cases, the invalidity of an interest may, under the *doctrine of infectious invalidity*, be held to invalidate one or more otherwise valid interests created by the disposition, or even invalidate the entire disposition. The question turns on whether the general dispositive scheme of the transferor will be better carried out by elimination of only the invalid interest or by elimination of other interests as well.

This is a question that must be answered on a case by case basis. Several items are relevant to the question, including who takes the stricken interests in place of the persons designated by the transferor. Some jurisdictions have become noted for a greater willingness to apply infectious invalidity than others. The following example is loosely based on *Taylor v. Dooley*, 297 S.W.2d 905 (Ky. 1956).

Example 5.16: G was survived by his two children, *A* and *B*. *G*'s will divided his property in half, devising one half to *A* outright and the other half "to *B* for life, then to *B*'s children who live to the age of 30."

The remainder in *B*'s children is invalid. The usual response would be to strike the remainder, thus creating an undisposed-of interest that would pass at *G*'s death to his heirs, presumably *A* and *B*. This would have the effect of increasing *A*'s eventual share to three fourths and reducing the share passing to *B*'s successors (presumably her children) to one fourth. Rather than permit this sizeable inequality, a court might conclude that it would be more consistent with *G*'s intention to apply the doctrine of infectious invalidity, striking all gifts created by the will, thus causing *G*'s property to pass by intestacy to *A* and *B* equally.

§ 5.11   Policy of the Rule

What is the purpose of the Rule Against Perpetuities? Professor Lewis Simes tackled this question in his article on The Policy Against Perpetuities, 103 U. Pa. L. Rev. 707 (1955). Simes identified four public policies that have been used to justify the Rule: (1) furthering the alienability of property, (2) enhancing the productivity of property, (3) preventing undue concentrations of wealth, and (4) prohibiting excessive dead-hand control. Simes argued, correctly, that the first two of these policies have little force in the modern era, because future interests are now mainly created in trusts, not directly in land (recall § 1.4). The trustee has the power to sell and reinvest trust assets, and the duty to make trust assets productive. The third of these policies also has less force, because we use (or can use) federal transfer taxation to limit wealth concentration. The fourth policy is the one that remains in force. In the words of Professor Simes, "the Rule Against Perpetuities strikes a fair balance between the desires of members of the present generation, and similar desires of succeeding generations, to do what they wish with the property which they enjoy." (For a critique, see T.P. Gallanis, The Rule Against Perpetuities and the Law Commission's Flawed Philosophy, 59 Camb. L. J. 284 (2000).)

Where is this "fair balance" to be drawn? Sir Arthur Hobhouse suggested a know-and-see theory: "A clear, obvious, natural line is drawn for us between those persons and events which the Settlor knows and sees, and those which he cannot know or see." Arthur Hobhouse, The Dead Hand 188 (1880). Professors Leach and Tudor expanded on the know-and-see test: "In a will a man of property could provide for all of those in his family whom he personally knew and the first generation after them upon attaining majority." W. Barton Leach & Owen Davies Tudor, The Common Law Rule Against Perpetuities, in Am. L. Prop. § 24.16. A further refinement of the theory has been suggested: "[T]he [know-and-see] standard [arguably means] that donors should be allowed to exert control through the youngest generation of descendants they knew and saw, or at least one or more but not necessarily all of whom they knew and saw." Lawrence W. Waggoner, The Uniform Statutory Rule Against Perpetuities, 21 Real. Prop., Prob. & Trust J. 569, 587 (1986).

As you study the material in this chapter, and especially as you work through the examples, keep in mind the know-and-see theory. Does the Rule effectively balance the interests of present and succeeding generations?

§ 5.12 Technical Violations

The required certainty that an interest will vest or terminate within a life in being plus 21 years has invalidated some interests even though they do not appear to violate the policy of the Rule. That is, the policy of the Rule would not seem to apply to such cases because, realistically speaking, the likelihood that the interest will remain contingent beyond the perpetuity period is remote. These cases have been labeled "technical violations." These cases fall generally into three categories, discussed in a famous article by Professor W. Barton Leach, Perpetuities in a Nutshell, 51 Harv. L. Rev. 638 (1938): (1) the fertile octogenarian, (2) the after-born spouse (termed by Leach the "unborn widow"), and (3) the administrative contingency.

The case of the fertile octogenarian refers to the Rule's presumption of lifetime fertility and how it interacts with the all-or-nothing rule of class gifts. Regardless of real-world facts, the Rule presumes that people are capable of having children until the moment of death. Yet the possibility of after-born children entering a class can be sufficient to render the class gift invalid. Consider the following example.

Example 5.17: G devised the residue of his estate in trust, directing the trustee to pay the income "to my daughter *A* for life, then to *A*'s children for the life of the survivor, and upon the death of *A*'s last surviving child, to pay the corpus of the trust to A's then-living grandchildren." G was survived by A and A's two children, X and Y.

The remainder in A's grandchildren is invalid because of the possibility that A might have a third child, Z, who might have a child (a grandchild of A) conceived and born more than 21 years after the death of the lives in being: A, X, and Y.

What if, in this example, the possibility of A having a third child, Z, was zero, because A was infertile having passed the menopause, or because A had undergone a hysterectomy (or, if A had been male, a vasectomy)? The answer is that such facts are irrelevant to the common-law Rule Against Perpetuities. For purposes of the common-law Rule, early English decisions, of which *Jee v. Audley*, 1 Cox's Ch. Cas. 324, 29 Eng. Rep. 1186 (Ch. 1787), is the best known, laid down the proposition that all persons are conclusively presumed to be capable of having children throughout their lifetimes, regardless of age or physical condition. In that case, Sir Lloyd Kenyon, the Master of the Rolls, stated:

> I am desired to do in this case something which I do not feel myself at liberty to do,

namely to suppose it impossible for persons in so advanced an age as John and Elizabeth Jee [both age 70] to have children; but if this can be done in one case it may in another, and it is a very dangerous experiment, and introductive of the greatest inconvenience to give a latitude to such sort of conjecture.

This presumption of lifetime fertility makes more sense than might originally appear. In the modern era, one must also consider the possibility of having children by adoption. The trend in modern law is strongly in favor of including adopted children in class gifts (see, for example, Uniform Probate Code § 2-705), and even elderly or infirm people can adopt.

In some instances, a way around the fertile octogenarian problem might be found in perpetuity law's general constructional preference for validity. If the possibility of future children was remote when the transferor executed the document, a court might hold that the transferor never intended to include after-born or after-adopted children within the class gift. With such children excluded, the Rule's requirement of initial certainty would be met, and the class gift valid. It is worth noting, however, that this strategy depends on what the transferor knew at the time the document was executed. In Example 5.17, if *A* were a 25-year old female in good physical condition when *G* signed the will, it would be hard to claim that *G* intended to exclude after-born or after-adopted children. It is also worth noting that some courts have been unwilling to use the general constructional preference for validity to overcome fertile octogenarian problems.

If adults are conclusively presumed to be able to have children, are children below the age of puberty (referred to by Professor Leach as "precocious toddlers") also subject to this presumption? Cases raising this question are rare, but they do seem to extend the presumption of fertility to one's entire lifetime. See *Rust v. Rust*, 147 Tex. 181, 211 S.W.2d 262, aff'd, 214 S.W.2d 246 (1948) (court assumed for perpetuity purposes that a 9-year old daughter would be able to have a child before her 14th birthday).

The second technical violation arises in the case of the after-born spouse. This term refers to the fact that an unnamed "spouse," "surviving spouse," "widow," or "widower" is excluded from serving as the validating life, because such person *might* have been conceived and born after the creation of the interest. Consider the following example.

Example 5.18: G devised land "to my son *A* for life, remainder to his widow for life, remainder to *A*'s then-living descendants." *G* was survived by *A*, *A*'s wife *W*, and their adult children *X* and *Y*.

The remainder in *A*'s descendants is invalid. Though improbable, it is possible that *A*'s widow will not be *W* but someone born after *G*'s death, who thus cannot serve as a validating life.

In some cases, the general constructional preference for validity has been used to avoid the after-born spouse problem. When the dispositive language fairly allows, some courts have construed the reference to *A*'s "widow," "widower," "spouse," or "surviving spouse," as a reference to the person to whom *A* was married when the will was executed or when *G* died (in this example, *W*). Of course, this is easier to do with terms such as "spouse," "husband," or "wife," than with terms that import an element of survivorship such as "widow," "widower," or "surviving spouse."

The third technical violation arises in the case of the administrative contingency, which refers to the performance by a fiduciary (an executor or trustee) of some administrative function which *might* take more than 21 years. Typical examples are the completion of the probate of a will, the settlement of an estate, the payment of debts or taxes, the sale of estate assets, or the delivery of trust corpus on the termination of a trust. Consider the following example.

Example 5.19: G devised land "to my grandchildren, born before or after my death, who are living upon final distribution of my estate."

By the majority view, the grandchildren's interest is invalid. Though unlikely, there is a possibility that final distribution will not occur within 21 years after G's death. This possibility means that no life can validate the interest. Grandchildren may be conceived and born after G's death, and such after-born grandchildren may survive the final distribution of G's estate (or fail to do so) beyond 21 years after the deaths of the children and grandchildren in being at the creation of the interest.

As this example illustrates, the term "administrative contingency" is somewhat misleading. The term does not refer to the possibility that the administrative task will never be completed. Rather, it is accepted that the task will be completed, presumably because of the fiduciary's legal obligation to do so. The uncertainty is the length of time it might take to finish the job.

A minority of courts has devised an escape from the administrative contingency problem. These courts hold that the fiduciary's obligation is to complete the task within a reasonable time, meaning less than 21 years. The difficulty with this minority view is that it is a fiction to say that the settlement of an estate can *never* take more than 21 years without violating a fiduciary duty. While rare, there can be cases in which protracted and successive litigation over a multitude of issues legitimately ties up an estate for a very long time.

§ 5.13   Perpetuity Saving Clauses

The common-law Rule is less fearsome to practicing estate-planning lawyers than it is to law students and law graduates studying for the bar examination. This is not because lawyers have found that the Rule becomes more understandable with experience, although that is also true, but because they have discovered that they need not be greatly concerned about the Rule's effect on their clients' plans because they use perpetuity saving clauses.

A typical perpetuity saving clause might provide:

> The trust hereby created shall terminate in any event not later than 21 years after the death of the last survivor of my descendants who are in being at the time this instrument becomes effective, *and unless sooner terminated by the terms hereof, the trustee shall, at the termination of such period, make distribution to the persons then entitled to the income of this trust, and in the same shares and proportions as they are so entitled.*

Formulated and used properly, perpetuity saving clauses mean that no lawyer need ever fear that a trust or other property arrangement will violate the common-law Rule. These clauses do not typically govern the term of the trust; they operate as a back-stop just in case the actual term of the trust exceeds the time allotted by the saving clause. The part of the clause that establishes this period of time is called the *perpetuity-period component*. Saving clauses also contain a second component, called the *gift-over component*, that expressly creates a gift guaranteed to vest at the termination of the period established in the perpetuity-period component but only if the interests have neither vested nor terminated earlier in accordance with their primary terms. In the sample saving clause above, the perpetuity-period component is underlined, and the gift-over component is in italics.

It needs to be stressed that a saving clause measures off a true "perpetuity period." The persons designated in a saving clause must be kept track of in order to determine when the last surviving member of the group dies.

In most cases, the saving clause not only avoids a violation of the common-law Rule; it also, in a sense, over-insures the client's disposition against the possibility that the gift over will ever take effect. The period of time established by the perpetuity-period component usually provides a margin of safety, because most trusts terminate on their own before the end of the perpetuity period would be reached. The clause, therefore, is usually a formality that validates the disposition without affecting the substance of the disposition.

§ 5.14   Perpetuity Reform: Discrete Repair, Immediate Reformation, and Wait-and-See (Herein the Uniform Statutory Rule Against Perpetuities)

Before the perpetual-trust movement gained momentum (see § 5.15 below), reform of the common-law Rule was in full throttle. The goal of the reform movement was to preserve the policy of the common-law Rule but blunt its nonpurposive applications—cases in which it would strike down all or part of a perfectly reasonable trust or other disposition.

The need for perpetuity reform was not much in doubt, but controversy persisted about the method. Three basic methods were advanced: (1) discrete statutory repair of the technical violations discussed above in § 5.12, along with reduction of age contingencies to 21; (2) immediate reformation; and (3) wait-and-see, with deferred reformation (reformation only if an interest remains contingent at the expiration of the permissible vesting period).

In the 1990s, the third method—wait-and-see with deferred reformation—had become the dominant method, and may make a comeback if Congress acts to remove the perpetual-trust

incentive. The Uniform Statutory Rule Against
Perpetuities (Uniform Rule or USRAP), which is
incorporated into the Uniform Probate Code as Part
9 of Article II, was enacted in 54 percent of the
states, and still is in effect in 15 states—Arkansas,
California, Connecticut, Georgia, Indiana, Kansas,
Massachusetts, Minnesota, Montana, New Mexico,
North Dakota, Oregon, South Carolina, Tennessee,
and West Virginia.

§ 5.14.1   Discrete repair and immediate reformation

The *discrete statutory repair* method of
perpetuity reform is now in effect in only one
jurisdiction—New York. Under New York law: (1)
males below 14 and females below 13 or above 55
are presumed incapable of having children,
evidence is admissible regarding the actual
inability to bear children, and the possibility of
having a child by adoption is disregarded; (2) an
interest in the spouse of another person is
presumed to refer to a person living at the date the
Rule commences to run; (3) administrative
contingencies are presumed to be completed within
the perpetuity period; and (4) where an interest
would be invalid because it depends upon a person
attaining or failing to attain an age exceeding 21

years, the age shall be reduced to 21. N.Y. Est., Powers & Tr. Law §§ 9-1.2, 9-1.3.

A few states have enacted statutes authorizing or directing *immediate reformation* of dispositions that violate the common-law Rule. Oklahoma's statute (60 Okl. St. § 75) is representative:

> Any interest in real or personal property that would violate the rule against perpetuities shall be reformed, or construed within the limits of the rule, to give effect to the general intent of the creator of that interest whenever that general intent can be ascertained. This provision shall be liberally construed and applied to validate such interest to the fullest extent consistent with such ascertained intent.

The difficulty with immediate reformation is that it requires up-front litigation as a regular matter.

A far preferable approach is *wait-and-see with deferred reformation.*

§ 5.14.2   Wait-and-see   with deferred reformation

Under the common-law Rule, the validity of a future interest depends on the full array of possible post-creation events. Why not instead take actual post-creation events into account? Instead of invalidating an interest because of what *might* happen, waiting to see what *does* happen seems much more sensible. Known as the wait-and-see method of perpetuity reform, this approach has been advocated by the two preeminent national organizations concerned with law reform—the American Law Institute in the Restatement 2d of Property (1983) and the National Conference of Commissioners on Uniform State Laws in the Uniform Rule (1990).

Neither the Restatement 2d of Property nor the Uniform Rule alters what may be called the *validating* side of the common-law Rule. Dispositions that would have been valid under the common-law Rule remain valid. Practitioners under either wait-and-see regime can and should continue to use a traditional perpetuity saving clause. The wait-and-see element is applied only to interests that fall prey to the *invalidating* side of the common-law Rule. Interests that would be invalid at common law are saved from being rendered *initially invalid*. To prevent the unjust enrichment of unintended takers caused by a drafter's mistake in failing to insert an appropriate perpetuity saving clause, otherwise invalid interests are, as it were, given a second chance: these interests are valid if they actually vest within the permissible vesting period and become invalid only if they remain in existence but still contingent at the expiration of that period.

Wait-and-see should be thought of as a perpetuity saving clause injected by law. The permissible vesting period under wait-and-see is, or should be, the equivalent of the perpetuity-period component of a well-conceived saving clause. Recall, too, that the saving clause includes a gift-over component. Deferred reformation is the near-equivalent, providing for judicial reformation of a disposition in case the interest is still in existence but contingent when the permissible vesting period expires.

Shifting the focus from possible to actual post-creation events has great attraction, and wait-and-see has been widely adopted, though still opposed by a few academics. The greatest controversy over wait-and-see concerns how the permissible vesting period is to be marked off—the permissible period of time for the contingencies attached to an otherwise invalid interest to be finally resolved.

The Restatement 2d of Property § 1.3(2) used a predetermined list of measuring lives. The permissible vesting period expires 21 years after the death of the survivor of:

(a) The transferor if the period of the rule begins to run in the transferor's lifetime; and

(b) Those individuals alive when the period of the rule begins to run, if reasonable in number, who have beneficial interests vested or contingent in the property in which the non-vested interest in question exists and the parents and grandparents alive when the period of the rule begins to run of all beneficiaries of the property in which the non-vested interest exists; and

(c) The donee of a nonfiduciary power of appointment alive when the period of the rule begins to run if the exercise of such power could affect the non-vested interest in question.

If a property interest is still in existence but contingent at the expiration of the permissible vesting period, Restatement 2d of Property § 1.5 provides that "the transferred property shall be disposed of in the manner which most closely effectuates the transferor's manifested plan of distribution and which is within the limits of the rule against perpetuities."

The Restatement 2d's version of wait-and-see has not been directly adopted by any court or legislature, although it did influence a provision of Iowa law. See Iowa Code § 558.68.

The general contour of the Uniform Rule is similar to that of the Restatement 2d of Property. The validating side of the common-law Rule is retained but the invalidating side is replaced with wait-and-see and deferred-reformation elements. The major departure from the Restatement 2d approach is that the Uniform Rule uses a flat 90-year vesting period, rather than a period ending 21 years after the death of the survivor of a predetermined list of measuring lives.

At the heart of the Uniform Rule is § 1(a):

> A nonvested property interest is invalid unless: (1) when the interest is created, it is certain to vest or terminate no later than 21 years after the death of an individual then alive; or (2) the interest either vests or terminates within 90 years after its creation.

Interests that are invalid under the Uniform Rule are subject to reformation under § 3, which provides:

> Upon the petition of an interested person, a court shall reform a disposition in the manner that most closely approximates the transferor's manifested plan of distribution and is within the 90 years allowed by [§ 1(a)] if: (1) a nonvested property interest or a power of appointment becomes invalid under [§ 1]; (2) a class gift is not but might become invalid under [§ 1] and the time has arrived when the share of any class member is to take effect in possession or enjoyment; or (3) a nonvested property interest that is not validated by [§ 1(a)] can vest but not within 90 years after its creation.

The most striking feature of the Uniform Rule is its use of a flat period of 90 years as the vesting period in its wait-and-see element. The rationale for this step was explained by the Reporter for the Uniform Rule, as follows:

> [T]he philosophy behind the 90-year period was to fix a period of time that

approximates the average period of time that would traditionally be allowed by the wait-and-see doctrine. There was no intention to use the flat-period-of-years method as a means of lengthening the [permissible vesting] period beyond its traditional boundaries. The fact that the traditional period roughly averages out to a longish-sounding 90 years is a reflection of a quite different phenomenon: the dramatic increase in longevity that society as a whole has experienced in the course of the twentieth century....

[T]he traditional method of delimiting the [permissible vesting] period [under earlier proposals for wait-and-see, including that of the Restatement 2d of Property] is to use actual measuring lives plus 21 years. Specifically, under this method, a group of persons—called the measuring lives—is identified. Once the group is identified, the lives of all its members are traced to see which one outlives all the others and when that survivor dies. The [permissible vesting] period extends 21 years beyond the death of that last surviving measuring life.

From its inception, the actual-measuring-lives approach has been plagued by two problems: identification and tracing. The identification problem concerns the method by which the measuring lives are to be chosen.... The second problem plaguing the actual-measuring-lives approach is that of tracing. No matter how the measuring lives are identified, the lives of those actual individuals must be traced to determine which one is the longest survivor and when he or she died....

By opting for a flat period of years, the framers of [the Uniform Rule] eliminated the clutter that has heretofore plagued the wait-and-see strategy—the problems of identifying, tracing, and possibly litigating the make-up of a sometimes-fluctuating group of measuring lives. The expiration of a [permissible vesting] period measured by a flat period of years is litigation free, easy to determine, and unmistakable....

In the normal course of events, the youngest measuring life is the key to the length of the [permissible vesting] period, and no matter which method is used for determining the identity of the measuring lives, the youngest measuring life, in standard trusts, is likely to be the transferor's youngest descendant living when the trust was created. The 90-year period of [the Uniform Rule] is premised on this proposition. Using four hypothetical families deemed to be representative of actual families, the framers determined that, on average, the transferor's youngest descendant in being at the transferor's death—assuming the transferor's death to occur between ages 60 and 90, which is when 73 percent of the population die—is about 6 years old. The remaining life expectancy of a 6-year old is about 69 years. The 69 years, plus the 21-year tack-on period, gives [a permissible vesting] period of 90 years. Although this method may not be scientifically accurate to the nth degree, the Drafting Committee considered it reliable enough to support a [permissible vesting] period of 90 years, given the margin-of-safety function that it performs.

Lawrence W. Waggoner, The Uniform Statutory Rule Against Perpetuities: The Rationale of the 90-Year Waiting Period, 73 Cornell L. Rev. 157, 162-68 (1988)(excerpted with the permission of the Cornell Law Review).

Section 3 of the Uniform Rule directs a court, upon the petition of an interested person, to reform a disposition within the limits of the 90-year permissible vesting period, in the manner deemed by the court most closely to approximate the transferor's manifested plan of distribution. The "interested person" who would frequently bring the reformation suit would be the trustee. Seldom will this section become operative. Of the fraction of trusts and other property arrangements that are incompetently drafted, and thus fail to meet the requirement of initial validity under the codified version of the validating side of the common-law Rule, almost all of them will have terminated by their own terms long before any of the circumstances requisite to reformation under § 3 arise.

If, against the odds, the right to reformation does arise, it will be found easier than perhaps anticipated to determine how best to reform the disposition. Note that reformation under § 3 is mandatory, not subject to the discretion of the court. Consequently, the common-law doctrine of infectious invalidity is superseded by the Uniform Rule. The court is given two reformation criteria: (1) the transferor's manifested plan of distribution, and (2) the 90-year permissible vesting period. Because governing instruments are where transferors manifest their plans of distribution, the imaginary horrible of courts being forced to probe the minds of long-dead transferors will not materialize.

The theory of § 3 is to defer the right to reformation until reformation becomes truly necessary. Thus, the basic rule of § 3(1) is that the right to reformation does not arise until a contingent property interest or a power of appointment becomes invalid; under § 1, this does not occur until the expiration of the 90-year permissible vesting period. By confining perpetuity litigation to those few cases in which the permissible vesting period actually is exceeded, perpetuity litigation is limited.

Example 5.20: G devised the residue of his estate in trust, directing the trustee to pay the income "to my daughter *A* for life, then to *A*'s children for the life of the survivor, and upon the death of *A*'s last surviving child, to pay the corpus of the trust to *A*'s then-living descendants, by representation."

The Uniform Rule allows 90 years for the remainder to vest. If *A* still has one or more living children on the 90th anniversary of *G*'s death, the remainder interest becomes invalid. However, the disposition can be judicially reformed to make it valid.

The most appropriate form of reformation would be to vest the remainder interest in *A*'s descendants who would take if *A*'s last surviving child had died on the 90th anniversary of *G*'s death. This would not cut short the income interest of *A*'s living children. The remainder in *A*'s descendants would be vested in interest but not in possession. Possession would still be postponed until the actual death of *A*'s last surviving child.

In certain cases, the Uniform Rule grants the right to reformation *before* the 90-year period runs out. The Uniform Rule grants a right to early reformation when it becomes necessary to do so or when there is no point in waiting that period out. Thus, the Uniform Rule in § 3(2) grants a right to early reformation whenever the share of any class member is entitled to take effect in possession or enjoyment, even though the class gift is not yet but might still become invalid under wait-and-see.

Example 5.21: G devised property in trust, directing the trustee to pay the income "to my son A for life, then to A's children"; the corpus of the trust is to be equally divided among A's children who reach the age of 30. G was survived by A and by A's two children X and Y, both of whom were under 30 when G died. After G's death, A had a third child, Z. Z's age was such that he could be alive but under age 30 on the 90th anniversary of G's death. At A's death, X and Y were over age 30.

The criteria for early reformation are met: (1) X and Y are entitled to possession of their shares as of A's death; and (2) under the all-or-nothing rule applicable to class gifts, the class gift might become invalid because Z might reach 30 beyond the 90-year period after G's death.

The most appropriate form of reformation would be to make Z's interest contingent on reaching, not age 30, but the 90th anniversary of G's death. This makes Z's interest valid under the Uniform Rule and validates the entire class gift. Under this approach, X and Y are immediately entitled to receive their one-third shares. If *Z*'s interest later vests, *Z* would receive the remaining one-third share. If *Z* fails to reach the 90th anniversary of *G*'s death, the one-third share would instead be divided equally between *X* and *Y* or their successors.

The Uniform Rule also grants the right to early reformation in one other situation: if a contingent property interest can vest but not before the 90-year period has expired. Though unlikely, such a case can theoretically arise. If it does, the interest—unless it terminates by its own terms earlier—is bound to become invalid under § 1 eventually. There is no point in deferring the right to reformation until the inevitable happens. The Uniform Rule provides for early reformation in such an event, just in case it arises. Consider the following example.

Example 5.22: *G* devised the residue of his estate in trust, directing the trustee to divide the income, by representation, among *G*'s descendants living from time to time, for 100 years. At the end of the 100 years, the trustee is to distribute the corpus to *G*'s then-living descendants, by representation.

Because the remainder interest in *G*'s descendants living 100 years after *G*'s death can vest but not before 90 years, the Uniform Rule grants a right to early reformation. The most appropriate form of reformation would be to reduce the 100-year period to 90 years.

§ 5.15 The Perpetual-Trust Movement

A few states had abolished (or had never adopted) the common-law Rule Against Perpetuities before 1986—including Wisconsin, South Dakota, and Idaho—but transferors had little desire to take advantage of the absence of the Rule in those states in order to establish perpetual trusts for their descendants from time to time living forever. After all, a transferor's genetic overlap with his or her descendants is cut in half at each succeeding generation. Specifically, a transferor's genetic overlap with his or her children is 50%, with his or her grandchildren is 25%, and with his or her great-grandchildren is 12.5%.[9] With four-generation families becoming more and more common due to increased longevity, an aging

---

[9]The 50% genetic overlap between a transferor and his or her children is precise; the genetic overlap between a transferor and his or her more remote descendants is an average. See John H. Beckstrom, Sociobiology and Intestate Wealth Transfers, 76 Nw. U. L. Rev. 216, 232 (1981).

transferor might live long enough to know and see some or all of his or her great-grandchildren, but as infants, not as adults. Seldom did a transferor think beyond great-grandchildren and contemplate benefiting more remote generations.

The federal generation-skipping transfer tax (GSTT) changed all that. Restated in 1986, the GSTT spurred a growing movement for states to abolish the Rule Against Perpetuities in order to allow perpetual trusts. The number of states abolishing the Rule in the years after 1986 has grown rapidly. Why is this so, given that the GSTT imposes high taxes on trusts that persist through more than one generation? The answer is that the GSTT also contains a large exemption—in 2013, $5.25 million per donor, and $10.5 million for married donors acting together.

In fashioning the GSTT exemption, Congress made a mistake: it relied on state perpetuity law to control the length of GSTT-exempt trusts. This mistake put the duration of GSTT-exempt trusts in the hands of the states, whose interest is more in generating trust business for its institutional trustees than in protecting the federal fisc. Hence was born a movement to abolish the Rule Against Perpetuities, or at least to modify it to permit trusts of hundreds of years. The movement began slowly, but accelerated as local lawyers and banking institutions in state after state learned of the potential for attracting trust business that the GSTT-exempt perpetual trust provided.

Despite the growing GSTT-exempt perpetual-trust movement, Congress has been complacent. Congress has not acted to curb the duration of the GSTT-exemption—not yet, anyway.

Eighteen jurisdictions now allow perpetual trusts: Alaska, Delaware (for trusts of personal property), the District of Columbia, Idaho, Illinois, Maine, Maryland, Missouri, Nebraska, New Hampshire, New Jersey, North Carolina, Ohio, Pennsylvania, Rhode Island, South Dakota, Virginia, and Wisconsin.

Twelve jurisdictions allow trusts to last for a century or more: Alabama (360 years), Alaska (1,000 years for the exercise or termination of a nongeneral power of appointment), Arizona (500 years), Colorado (1,000 years), Delaware (100 years, for trusts of real property), Florida (360 years), Michigan (360 years), Nevada (365 years), Tennessee (360 years), Utah (1,000 years), Washington (150 years), and Wyoming (1,000 years).

Eight of the perpetual-trust or near-perpetual trust jurisdictions transform the Rule Against Perpetuities into a default rule. Settlors can opt out, but they have to do so expressly. The opt-out jurisdictions are the District of Columbia, Illinois, Maine, Maryland, Nebraska, New Hampshire, Ohio, and Virginia.

The function of a default rule (rule of construction) is to carry out intent. The Rule Against Perpetuities is a mandatory rule of law that purposely defeats intent on grounds of public policy. Changing an intent-defeating rule into a default rule is wrong-headed. See Restatement 3d of Property § 16.3 cmt. a.

Over time, a perpetual trust is likely to turn into an administrative nightmare. Government statistics indicate that the average married couple has about two children. If we assume that two children and four grandchildren are living at the settlor's death, that the interval between generations is 25 years, that three generations of descendants are living at any given time, and that the settlor and each member of the senior descendant generation dies at age 75, the following projections can be made. The average settlor will have about 450 descendants (who are beneficiaries of the trust) 150 years after the trust is created, over 7,000 beneficiaries 250 years after the trust is created, and about 114,5000 beneficiaries after 350 years. If we go 450 years, the number of living beneficiaries could rise to 1.8 million.

§ 5.16   The Rule Against Perpetuities Under the Restatement 3d of Property

In May 2010, the American Law Institute approved the final chapters of the Restatement 3d of Property, including Chapter 27 on the Rule Against Perpetuities. Chapter 27 contains two innovations.

First, Chapter 27 firmly states, as the official position of the American Law Institute, that the movement to allow perpetual or multiple-centuries trusts is ill advised:[10]

> It is the considered judgment of the American Law Institute that the recent statutory movement allowing the creation

[10]For discussion, see Lawrence. W. Waggoner, The Case for Curtailing Dead-Hand Control: The American Law Institute Declares the Perpetual-Trust Movement Ill Advised, University of Michigan Public Law Working Paper No. 199 (2010), available at http://ssrn.com/abstract =1614934.

of perpetual or multiple-centuries trusts is ill advised. The movement to abrogate the Rule Against Perpetuities has not been based on the merits of removing its curb on excessive dead-hand control. The policy issues associated with allowing perpetual or multiple-centuries trusts have not been seriously discussed in the legislatures. The driving force has been the effort to take some trust industry (financial services) jobs from other states.

A rule that curbs excessive dead-hand control is deeply rooted in this nation's history and tradition, and for good reason. A 360-year trust created in the year 2010 could endure until the year 2370 had have over 100,000 beneficiaries. A 1000-year trust created in 2010 could terminate in the year 3010 and have millions of beneficiaries.   No transferor has enough wisdom to make sound dispositions of property across such vast intervals and for beneficiaries so remote and so numerous. A 1000-year or 360-year trust created in 2010 might incorporate what are currently considered to be flexible provisions for a trust that could last that far into the future.

To put that claim into perspective, consider the devices for controlling family wealth through subsequent generations that were available 360 or more years ago, in the year 1650 or earlier. Such devices, drafted before the invention of the typewriter, first took the form of the unbarrable entail and, after the entail became barrable, the strict settlement. These devices became archaic long ago. If that which was considered sophisticated 360 or more years ago is considered primitive today, there is reason to suspect that that which is considered sophisticated today will be considered primitive 360 or more years from now.

Restatement 3d of Property ch. 27, Introductory Note.

Second, Chapter 27 reformulates the Rule Against Perpetuities. The Rule is no longer a rule against the remote vesting of contingent future interests, measured by lives in being. Instead, the Rule concerns the time of the interest's termination.[11] The Rule provides that a trust or other donative disposition of property is subject to judicial modification to the extent that the trust or other disposition does not terminate on or before the expiration of the perpetuity period. The perpetuity period is limited to the lives of individuals no more than two generations younger than the transferor.[12]

Below are the relevant provisions from the Restatement 3d:

§ 27.1   Statement of the Rule Against Perpetuities

(a) A trust or other donative disposition

---

[11]For the idea of changing the Rule to require termination on or before the expiration of a perpetuity period, see Daniel M. Schuyler, Should the Rule Against Perpetuities Discard Its Vest?, 56 Mich. L. Rev. 683 (1958); Thomas P. Gallanis, The Future of Future Interests, 60 Wash. & Lee. L. Rev. 513, 559-60 (2003).

[12]For discussion, see Lawrence W. Waggoner, The American Law Institute Proposes a New Approach to Perpetuities: Limiting the Dead Hand to Two Younger Generations, University of Michigan Public Law Working Paper No. 200 (2010), available at http://ssrn.com/abstract=1614936.

of property is subject to judicial
modification under § 27.2 to the extent
that the trust or other disposition does not
terminate on or before the expiration of
the perpetuity period, except that if, upon
the expiration of the perpetuity period, the
share of a beneficiary is distributable on
reaching a specified age and the
beneficiary is then younger than the
earlier of the specified age or the age of
30, the beneficiary's share may, without
judicial modification, be retained in trust
until the beneficiary reaches or dies
before reaching the earlier of the specified
age or the age of 30.

(b) The perpetuity period expires at the
death of the last living measuring life.
The measuring lives are as follows:

(1) Except as otherwise provided in
paragraph (2), the measuring lives
constitute a group composed of the
following individuals: the transferor, the
beneficiaries of the disposition who are
related to the transferor and no more than
two generations younger than the
transferor, and the beneficiaries of the

disposition who are unrelated to the transferor and no more than the equivalent of two generations younger than the transferor.

(2) In the case of a trust or other property arrangement for the sole current benefit of a named individual who is more than two generations younger than the transferor or more than the equivalent of two generations younger than the transferor, the measuring life is the named individual....

[Comment] f. Beneficiaries who are unrelated to the transferor who can be subsection (b)(1) measuring lives.... This Restatement refers to the federal generation-skipping transfer tax (GST tax) to determine whether an unrelated beneficiary is no more than the equivalent of two generations younger than the transferor. Currently, the GST tax assigns an unrelated beneficiary on the basis of the age difference between the beneficiary and the transferor. IRC § 2651(d) provides that such an individual is "assigned to a generation on the basis of

the date of such individual's birth with —
(1) an individual born not more than 12½
years after the date of the birth of the
transferor assigned to the transferor's
generation, (2) an individual born more
than 12½ years but not more than 37½
years after the date of the birth of the
transferor assigned to the first generation
younger than the transferor, and (3)
similar rules for a new generation every
25 years."...

§ 27.2 Judicial Modification

Upon the petition of an interested
person, the court shall modify a
disposition that is subject to judicial
modification under § 27.1(a). The form of
the modification must be in a manner than
most closely approximates the
transferor's manifested plan of
distribution and is within the perpetuity
period provided in § 27.1(b).

To see how the reformulated Rule Against
Perpetuities compares to the common-law Rule,
consider the following examples.

Example 5.23: G devised property "to my son *A* for life, then to *A*'s children from time to time living for the life of the survivor, and on the death of *A*'s last surviving child, to *A*'s then living descendants." *G* was survived by *A* and by *A*'s two children, *X* and *Y*. After *G*'s death, *A* had another child, *Z*. *A*, *X*, and *Y* are now dead, survived by *Z*.

At common law, the contingent remainder for life in *A*'s children is valid under the Rule (*A* is the validating life), but there is no validating life for the contingent remainder in fee in *A*'s descendants. That remainder is stricken from the disposition. Thus, at the death of *A*'s last surviving child (*Z*), the property will revert to *G*—meaning *G*'s successors in interest. *G*'s estate will need to be re-opened in order to identify them.

Under the reformulated Rule, *G*'s devise is valid. The remainder interest in *A*'s descendants will terminate before the death of the last living measuring life. The measuring lives here are *G*'s grandchildren (*A*'s children). They are beneficiaries of the disposition who are no more than two generations younger than the transferor (*G*). Once *G*'s last grandchild (*A*'s last child, *Z*) dies, the disposition will

Uniform Rule, and the reformula
the Restatement 3d of Property, a
valid.

The rationale for this exemption
allows property to be tied up pe
single charity, so it ought to ac
treatment to shifts from one charit

It should also be noted that, where
does not apply because the prece
noncharitable, there is a pronounc
the case law to construe the charit
vested if the dispositive languag
construction. Many charitable inter
invalid, have been saved by this
device.

With respect to commercial tran
contracts create property interests t
to the common-law Rule. Exam
interests include options in gross,
refusal, and leases scheduled to co
future. At common law, such inter
if they are exercisable beyond a lif
21 years. The perpetuity argument i:
by the party seeking to avoid perfor
her part of the contract.

terminate by its own terms, and the property
will be distributed to *A*'s then-living
descendants.

Example 5.24: *G* devised property in trust,
directing the trustee to distribute the income at
the trustee's discretion among *G*'s descendants
from time to time living. The terms of the trust
require the trust to terminate when *G* no longer
has any living descendants. On termination of
the trust, the trustee is directed to distribute the
trust principal to a specified charity. At *G*'s
death, *G* had two adult children, *C1* and *C2*,
and four adult grandchildren, *GC1*, *GC2*, *GC3*,
and *GC4*. No grandchildren of *G* were born or
adopted after *G*'s death. *G*'s grandchildren died
in numerical order—*GC1*, then *GC2*, then
GC3, and then *GC4*. At *GC4*'s death (at age
88), *G* had 50 living descendants: eight great-
grandchildren, 16 great-great-grandchildren,
and 26 great-great-great grandchildren.

The trust is subject to judicial modification
under § 27.2, because the trust did not
terminate on or before the expiration of the
perpetuity period. The perpetuity period
expired on the death of *G*'s last surviving
grandchild—*GC4*. The court should modify the
trust by requiring it to terminate at *GC4*'s death

and should order the trust
distributed by represent
descendants living when the
expired.

§ 5.17   A Special Note on
and Commercial Tr:

This section discusses the appl
Against Perpetuities to chai
commercial transactions.

Future interests created in chai
the common-law Rule, the Unif
reformulated Rule under the R
Property in the same way as futui
in private parties, with one
exception concerns future interes
are preceded by an interest ci
charity. In such a case, the fu
charity will not be subject to the F
following example.

Example 5.25: G devised lar
as long as the land is used
purposes, and upon the cessatio
Y Charity."

The executory interest creat(
is exempt from the common

An *option in gross* is a contract right to purchase property held by an optionee who has no possessory interest in the property. If the subject of an option is land or a unique chattel, the option is specifically enforceable. Specifically enforceable contracts are treated as creating equitable property interests. Since equitable property interests are subject to the common-law Rule, the great majority view at common law is that options in gross are invalid if they are exercisable beyond a life in being plus 21 years.

Example 5.26: (1) A, the owner of Blackacre, sells an option to *B* under which *A* obligates himself and his heirs and assigns to convey Blackacre at any time in the future to *B* and her heirs and assigns, for $X.00.

(2) A, the owner of Blackacre, sells Blackacre to *B*. As part of the transaction, *B* obligates herself and her heirs and assigns to reconvey Blackacre at any time in the future to *A* and his heirs and assigns for $X.00.

The great majority view at common law is that both options are invalid. This means that neither option is specifically enforceable and that damages are not recoverable for its breach.

Note that the option in Variation (2) was reserved by the transferor. Although reversionary interests are not subject to the Rule, reserved options are not granted the same immunity. See *Woodall v. Bruen*, 76 W.Va. 153, 85 S.E. 170 (1915).[13] Yet the difference between a reserved option and a right of entry may only be a matter of form. Suppose the grant in Variation (2) had read "to *B* and her heirs, but if the grantor or his heirs should ever tender $X.00 to *B* or her heirs or assigns, the grantor or his heirs shall have the right to re-enter and retake the premises." Presumably this change in form would transform *A*'s invalid option into a valid right of entry.

Options that expire if they are not exercised within a life in being plus 21 years are valid. The options in the preceding example would have been valid at common law if the owner's obligation to sell had been limited to "the lifetime of the survivor of *A* and *B*," or to "the next 21 years," or to some other period within the Rule. Even if not explicitly so limited, a court might construe the language of the option as being so limited. The absence of language such as "his/her heirs and

[13]West Virginia subsequently enacted the Uniform Rule, including its exemption of commercial transactions.

assigns," for instance, might lead a court to hold that the option was to last only during the lifetime of either party or only during their joint lives.

Unlike options to purchase, *rights of first refusal* do not obligate the owner to sell. They only obligate the owner to offer the property first to the preemptioner if the owner decides to sell. The preemptioner can buy or decline. If the preemptioner declines, the owner is then free to sell to anyone else. Rights of first refusal have been held to be subject to the common-law Rule, and void if they are exercisable beyond a life in being plus 21 years. See *Ferrero Const. Co. v. Dennis Rourke Corp.*, 311 Md. 560, 536 A.2d 1137 (1988).

A *lease scheduled to commence in the future* is invalid if it is subject to a contingency that might occur beyond a life in being plus 21 years. There has been considerable litigation concerning so-called "on-completion" leases—leases scheduled to commence when construction of a building is completed. On-completion leases would clearly be valid if the lessor was obligated to complete construction within 21 years, but in the absence of an obligation of this sort, some courts have held the lease to be invalid. See *Southern Airways Co. v. DeKalb County*, 102 Ga.App. 850, 118 S.E.2d

234 (1960)(rev'd on other grounds). Other courts, though, have upheld such leases on the theory that the lessee's interest was vested from the beginning, see *Isen v. Giant Food Inc.*, 295 F.2d 136 (D.C. Cir. 1961), or that there was an implicit obligation to complete the building within a reasonable time, see *Singer Co. v. Makad Inc.*, 213 Kan. 725, 518 P.2d 493 (1974).

In our view, the Rule Against Perpetuities is an inappropriate tool of social policy with respect to such transactions. The perpetuity period makes sense as a limit on donative transfers of property but is unsuitable for bargained-for exchanges. Agreeing with this perspective, the Uniform Rule provides in § 4(1)—and the Restatement 3d of Property provides in § 27.3—that commercial transactions are excluded from the Rule. Another approach taken by some states is to enact statutory provisions limiting the duration of certain commercial transactions to a flat number of years. See 765 Ill. Comp. Stat. 305/4; Mass. Gen. Laws ch. 184A, § 5.

CHAPTER 6

THREE OTHER RULES
GOVERNING FUTURE INTERESTS

This chapter covers three rules of future interest law that remain in force in some U.S. states. Law students should be aware of these rules, which remain as traps for the unwary. The rules are: (1) the rule of the destructibility of contingent remainders; (2) the Rule in Shelley's Case; and (3) the doctrine of worthier title.

§ 6.1 The Rule of the Destructibility of Contingent Remainders

The *rule of the destructibility of contingent remainders*, known in shorthand as the "destructibility rule," dates from the late sixteenth century. It provides that *a legal contingent remainder (meaning a contingent remainder*

*directly in land rather than in a trust) is destroyed
if it does not vest by the time the preceding
freehold estate terminates.* The rule does not apply
(1) to vested remainders, even if the remainder is
vested subject to divestment; (2) to executory
interests; (3) to contingent remainders in personal
property; (4) to equitable contingent remainders,
meaning contingent remainders in a trust, even if
land is a trust asset; or (5) to contingent remainders
if the preceding estate is nonfreehold, such as a
term of years.

The best way to understand the rule is to see it in
operation, as in the following example.

Example 6.1: G transferred land "to *A* for
life, remainder to *B* if *B* lives to age 21." At *A*'s
death, *B* is under age 21.

At *A*'s death, *B*'s remainder is still contingent,
because we do not yet know whether *B* will live to
age 21. Accordingly, *G*'s reversion operates. In a
jurisdiction without the destructibility rule, *G*'s
reversion vests in possession as a defeasible fee
subject to *B*'s interest, now no longer a contingent
remainder but instead an executory interest. In a
jurisdiction with the destructibility rule, *G*'s
reversion vests in possession as a fee simple
absolute; *B*'s contingent remainder, instead of

becoming an executory interest, is destroyed. Note that this result occurs irrespective of *G*'s intention. The destructibility rule is a mandatory rule of law, not a default rule of construction.

The case of *Purefoy v. Rogers*, 85 Eng. Rep. 1181 (K.B. 1671), presented an opportunity for the common-law courts to save contingent remainders such as *B*'s by declaring that the remainder could change into an executory interest. But this was not to be. The judges in *Purefoy v. Rogers* declared that a contingent remainder cannot avoid destruction by changing into an executory interest:

> [F]or where a contingency is limited to depend on an estate of freehold which is capable of supporting a remainder, it shall never be construed to be an executory devise, but a contingent remainder only, and not otherwise.

The destructibility rule has its origins in the English feudal system before the Statute of Uses. In that system, the transfer of land from one person to another meant the transfer of seisin, or the right to possess the land. In the prototypical transfer with a future interest—*G* transfers land "to *A* for life, remainder to *B*"—seisin would pass initially from *G* to *A*. Under a legal fiction accepted at common law, *A* would hold seisin for himself and for *B*, and at *A*'s death seisin would pass to *B*. But in Example 6.1, *B* has not, at *A*'s death, satisfied the condition precedent to possession and thus would not be capable of accepting seisin, thereby triggering a reversion to *G*. Yet *G* would hold seisin for himself only, because English law did not permit the holder of an interest in fee simple to hold seisin partly on behalf of another. Only the holder of a freehold interest *less* than fee simple (such as a life estate) could do so. Accordingly, *G*'s reversion vesting in possession as a fee simple would give seisin to *G* alone, and *B*'s contingent remainder would be destroyed.

The destructibility rule never applied to executory interests, because the Statute of Uses enabled seisin to shift (or spring) to the holder of such interests even without a preceding freehold estate for support. Put differently: the conceptual and legal structures that gave rise to the destructibility rule were altered by the Statute of Uses, with the result that executory interests were not subject to destruction.

Example 6.1 involved one typical scenario of destructibility: a *gap in time* between the termination of the freehold estate and the vesting of the remainder. There is also a second scenario in which the destructibility rule operated, involving the doctrine of *merger*. The doctrine of merger provides that *if, after creation, a life estate and a successive vested future interest in fee come into the hands of the same person, the life estate terminates by merging into the other interest.* Consider the following example.

Example 6.2: (1) G devised land "to *A* for life, remainder to *B* if *B* survives *A*." *G*'s will contains no residuary clause, and *G*'s sole heir is *R*.

(2) G devised land "to *A* for life, remainder to *B* if *B* survives *A*, but if not, to *C*." *G*'s will contains no residuary clause, and *G*'s sole heir is *R*.

In both cases, *R* has a reversion, albeit merely a technical one in Variation (2). If *R* conveys his reversion to *A*, *A*'s life estate will merge into the reversion, giving *A* a fee simple. If the destructibility rule is not in force, the merger would produce a fee simple defeasible, with the contingent remainders in *B* (and in Variation (2), in *C*) changing into executory interests. If the destructibility rule is in force, the merger would destroy the contingent remainders of *B* and *C*, giving *A* a fee simple absolute. Note that the same results would obtain if *A* had initially conveyed his life estate to *R*, rather than the reverse, or if both *A* and *R* had conveyed their interests to a third person.[1]

Whether triggered by time gap or merger,[2] the

---

[1]Suppose instead that *A* was sole heir, not *R*, meaning that at *G*'s death *A* received both the life estate and the reversion. Would they merge at that moment? No. A life estate and reversion created simultaneously in the same person (*A*) do not merge at creation if there is an intervening contingent remainder. But the interests will merge upon a post-creation transfer to a third party. For example, if *A* conveyed the life estate and reversion to a third party, *X*, the interests would merge and the contingent remainders of *B* (and in Variation (2), *C*) would be destroyed.

[2]The destructibility rule could also be triggered in England by *forfeiture*—for example, when a life tenant purported to convey a fee simple. The transferee would receive a "tortious fee," an estate in fee simple that was subject to a right of entry in the person holding the next vested estate, typically the reversioner. The fact that the transferee's estate was an estate in fee simple caused the destruction of any contingent remainder previously supported by the life estate.

Forfeiture of a life estate was never recognized in the United States. The American rule is that a person cannot convey more than he has (*nemo dat quod non habet*). Thus, a life tenant cannot convey more than a life estate.

rule of destructibility was a part of the common law and, as such, was received in American jurisdictions. Today, however, most states have abolished the rule by statute or abrogated it by judicial decision. In the remaining minority of states, the question is largely open, although the Restatement of Property § 240 takes the position that the rule is not part of American law. Accord Restatement 3d of Property § 25.5. Only in Florida can one find post-World War II decisions endorsing the rule. See *In re Estate of Rentz*, 152 So.2d 480 (Fla.App. 1963).

Is the destructibility rule a sound instrument of social policy? There is no doubt that legal contingent future interests hinder the free alienability of land. Contingent future interests are often created in a class that includes unborn or unascertained persons. Thus the destructibility rule might be seen as promoting the free alienability of property by destroying interests that cannot be transferred. One can speculate that this view of the destructibility rule accounted for the decision in *Purefoy v. Rogers*. It was also about this time that the first seeds of the Rule Against Perpetuities had begun to emerge.

In our view, however, the destructibility rule is a poor instrument of social policy. Its application is narrow (only legal contingent remainders in land following a freehold), hence the rule is easily avoided by careful drafting. In contrast, the Rule Against Perpetuities applies more widely: to executory interests as well as contingent remainders, to equitable interests as well as legal interests, and to personalty as well as to land.

§ 6.2　The Rule in Shelley's Case

The *Rule in Shelley's Case* derives its name from the case of *Wolfe v. Shelley*, 1 Co. Rep. 93b, 76 Eng. Rep. 206 (K.B. 1581). The rule itself, however, was recognized at least two centuries earlier. The rule provides that a remainder interest *in land in favor of the life tenant's heirs*[3] *is held by*

---

[3]For purposes of the Rule in Shelley's Case, most American jurisdictions interpret the word "heirs" in its standard sense: the persons who succeed to property if the owner dies intestate. A remainder in the life tenant's heirs so understood triggers the rule. A few American jurisdictions adopt a contrary view, holding that the rule applies only when heirs is understood in a different sense: an indefinite line including not just the first takers in intestacy (heirs in the standard sense) but also their heirs, their heirs' heirs, and so on forever. By way of example, a transfer by *G* "to *A* for life,

the life tenant. Note that this rule applies only to (1) remainders (2) in land (3) in favor of the heirs[4] (4) of the life tenant.[5] Consider the following example.

remainder to *A*'s heirs who are living at *A*'s death" would trigger the rule in most jurisdictions, because the extra wording merely restates the standard definition. But the rule would not be triggered in the jurisdictions requiring a remainder in an indefinite succession of generations, because that is not the remainder this particular grantor (*G*) created.

Even in the majority of jurisdictions, the remainder must be described in a way that is definitionally equal to the life tenant's "heirs." A remainder in the life tenant's "children" will not trigger the rule even if it turns out in fact that the life tenant's children are his only heirs. See Restatement 2d of Property § 30.1 cmt. g.

[4]The rule also applies to remainders in favor of the heirs of the life tenant's body, but this formulation is too rare in modern times to be worth discussing. See also § 2.5 on the status of the fee tail under American law.

[5]The rule does not apply if the prior estate is nonfreehold, such as a term of years. Accordingly, one device for avoiding the rule is to make the term of years much longer than *A*'s life expectancy and determinable on *A*'s earlier death: "to *A* for 150 years or until *A*'s death, then to *A*'s heirs." See Restatement 2d of Property § 39.1 cmt. c.

Example 6.3: (1) G transferred land "to *A* for life, remainder to *A*'s heirs."

(2) G transferred land "to *A* for the life of *X*, remainder to *A*'s heirs."

(3) G transferred land "to *X* for life, then to *A* for life, remainder to *A*'s heirs."

Without the Rule in Shelley's Case, *A* has an interest in the property for life, after which the property passes to *A*'s heirs. Applying the rule yields a very different result: *A* holds both an interest for life and the remainder in fee, which in this example is indefeasibly vested. On these facts, the doctrine of merger (explained in § 6.1) would apply, giving *A* the land in fee simple absolute in Variations (1) and (2) and giving *A* an indefeasibly vested remainder in Variation (3). Note that the Rule in Shelley's Case does not automatically trigger a merger; it merely gives the remainder interest to the life tenant. Merger occurs only if the independent requirements of the merger doctrine are met.

The application of the rule occurs without regard to what *G* intended when making the transfer. The Rule in Shelley's Case is an absolute rule of law, not a rule of construction that yields to an expression of contrary intent. Moreover, the rule governs transfers of land whether made outright or in trust, meaning that both legal and equitable remainders are subject to it.[6] The rule also applies equally to inter vivos and testamentary transfers of land. The rule does not apply to personalty.[7]

The traditional explanation for the rule points to the English feudal system. In that system, land was not devisable by will; instead, it descended to one's heirs at death. If we imagine Example 6.3 within a feudal system, the land would pass to *A*'s heirs no matter whether *A* owned a life estate or the entire property. The crucial distinction comes in the method of transfer. Without the rule, the heirs would take the land by purchase, meaning by the terms of *G*'s disposition; with the rule, the heirs would take by descent, meaning by operation of law. In the latter case, but not in the former, the

[6]The rule applies only where the life estate and the remainder are of the same quality, meaning that they must both be legal interests or both be equitable interests. If one is legal and the other equitable, the rule does not apply. See Restatement 2d of Property § 30.1(1) & cmt. h.

[7]An apparent exception is Ohio, where in *Society Nat'l Bank v. Jacobson*, 54 Ohio St.3d 15, 560 N.E.2d 217 (1990), the Ohio Supreme Court in a muddled opinion applied the Rule in Shelley's Case to personal property in trust.

feudal lord would be able to exact dues from the heirs before allowing them to receive the land. Thus, the explanation goes, the Rule in Shelley's Case protected lords and their revenue from attempts to evade feudal obligations.

The typical disposition triggering the rule is the one in Example 6.3, Variation (1): a transfer "to *A* for life, remainder to *A*'s heirs." Yet the rule can also be triggered on more complex facts.

Consider, for instance, the problem of fractional interests. Some cases have arisen in which the life estate and the remainder were of an undivided fraction of the whole. Little difficulty arises when the fractions correspond.

Example 6.4: G transferred land "to *A* and *B* equally for their respective lives, and on the death of each, *A*'s half to *A*'s heirs and *B*'s half to *B*'s heirs."

The Rule in Shelley's Case and the doctrine of merger combine to give *A* and *B* each an undivided half of the fee, probably as tenants in common rather than as joint tenants. See Restatement 2d of Property § 30.1 illus. 27.

Even when the fractions do not correspond, the applicability of the rule can still be determined.

Example 6.5: G transferred land "to A for life, remainder in half to B and in the other half to the heirs of A."

The Rule in Shelley's Case and the doctrine of merger combine to give A an undivided half in fee simple absolute; the other half is held by A for life, with the remainder in that half going to B.

Example 6.6: G transferred land "to A and B equally for life, and on the death of each, to the heirs of A."

A has only a life estate in half, so the Rule in Shelley's Case operates only on half of the remainder. The doctrine of merger then gives A a fee simple in that undivided half. The Rule in Shelley's Case does not apply to the other undivided half—the half in which B has a life estate. See Restatement of Property § 312 illus. 26

For an analysis of the result if the disposition had instead read "on the death *of the survivor,*" see Restatement of Property § 312 cmt. r.

The Rule in Shelley's Case can also be triggered by events that occur after the initial transfer, if the rule's requirements are subsequently satisfied and if the subsequent satisfaction comes about automatically in accordance with the terms of the original transfer. This can occur, for instance, if the future interest in the life tenant's heirs is transformed from an executory interest into a remainder, as in the following example.

Example 6.7: G transferred land "to A for life, remainder to B, but if B fails to survive A, to A's heirs." B later died, survived by A.

The Rule in Shelley's Case does not apply at the time of the initial transfer, because the future interest in A's heirs is an executory interest, not a remainder. At B's death, the interest becomes a remainder, at which point the Rule in Shelley's Case would apply, converting the remainder intended for A's heirs into a remainder in A. The doctrine of merger would then give A a fee simple absolute. See Restatement § 312 cmt. q; Restatement 2d of Property § 30.1 cmt. p. But see Simes & Smith on Future Interests § 1562 (arguing against post-creation application).

The rule will *not* be triggered by events other than the automatic application of the terms of the original transfer. For example, the rule will not apply if a life estate created in a third party later comes into the hands of the person whose heirs hold the remainder. See the following example.

Example 6.8: G transferred land "to B for life, remainder to the heirs of A." B later assigns her life interest to A.

The Rule in Shelley's Case does not apply, because the life estate was not originally created in the ancestor (A).

The Rule in Shelley's Case was abolished in England in 1925. In the United States, the rule has been abolished by statute or abrogated by judicial decision in most jurisdictions. It has also been repudiated by the American Law Institute. See Restatement 3d of Property § 16.2; Restatement 3d of Trusts § 49, cmt. a(1). The rule continues in force in a small number of jurisdictions, especially Arkansas and Delaware, where the rule has been invoked in judicial decisions as recently as the 1980s. See *Smith v. Wright*, 300 Ark. 416, 779 S.W.2d 177 (1989); *Estate of Donovan*, 1983 WL 103280 (Del. Ch. Apr. 14, 1983). It is also worth noting that statutes abolishing the rule are usually not retroactive, hence do not apply to pre-effective-date instruments.

Like the destructibility rule, the Rule in Shelley's Case might initially seem an instrument of social policy, promoting the alienability of land by enabling the life tenant to obtain a fee simple absolute. Yet the Rule in Shelley's Case operates in an even narrower range than the destructibility rule: only to remainders in the life tenant's heirs. This defect, combined with better solutions to the problem of inalienable land (see § 6.1), mean that the Rule in Shelley's Case cannot be justified as an instrument of social policy. See Restatement 3d of Property § 16.2 cmt. b.

§ 6.3   The Doctrine of Worthier Title

The *doctrine of worthier title* derives from England, where it emerged no later than the sixteenth century, and probably earlier. The doctrine provides that *a future interest*[8] *in the grantor's heirs*[9] *is to be treated as a future interest*

---

[8]The doctrine originally applied as rule of law to remainders in land. Expanded as a rule of construction, the doctrine applies equally to remainders and executory interests, whether legal or equitable, whether in land or in personalty. This is important, as most modern future interests are created in trusts of personalty.

[9]The divergent notion of an indefinite line of succession (see footnote 3) never crept into the worthier title doctrine. The doctrine is thus triggered by future interests in the grantor's heirs, understood as the persons who succeed to the grantor's intestate estate. Accordingly, a future interest in the

retained by the grantor. Consider the following example.

> *Example 6.9:* G transferred property "to A for life, remainder to G's heirs."

By the terms of the transfer, A receives an interest for life, after which the property passes to G's heirs. Applying the doctrine, however, the transfer is rewritten as "to A for life, reversion in G." The customary explanation for the worthier title doctrine is the same as the one traditionally offered for the Rule in Shelley's Case: both rules require heirs to take property by descent rather than by the terms of the transfer—title by descent being "worthier" than title by purchase—because only on descent could feudal lords exact the customary dues.

The doctrine was abolished in England in 1833 but continues to exist in a modified form in some parts of the United States. In order to understand

---

grantor's "next of kin" would trigger the doctrine if that term is definitionally the same as "heirs" under state law, whereas a future interest in the grantor's "children" or "descendants" would not (regardless of whether the grantor's children or descendants actually turn out to be his or her heirs at death).

the doctrine's current contours, it is necessary to recognize that the doctrine has split into two branches. The *testamentary branch* concerns transfers made by will; the *inter vivos branch* applies to transfers made during lifetime.

The doctrine's testamentary branch is virtually extinct in the United States. Of the 31 jurisdictions that have addressed the issue by statute or judicial decision, 30 have rejected it. The one outlier state is Maryland, where the state's highest court noted the testamentary branch in *Donnelly v. Turner*, 60 Md. 81 (1883); but no Maryland court has considered the question since then, so the continued existence of the testamentary branch there is doubtful. Moreover, the Restatement of Property § 314(2) and the Restatement 2d of Property § 30.2(2) have squarely rejected the testamentary branch, as has § 2-710 of the Uniform Probate Code. It is fair to say that the worthier title doctrine's testamentary branch is dead in the United States.

In contrast, the inter vivos branch still exists in some American jurisdictions, although very few. Most of the state statutes abolishing the testamentary branch also abolished the inter vivos branch, a notable exception being the statute in

Washington, which preserves the inter vivos branch as a rule of construction under certain circumstances. Wash. Rev. Code § 11.12.185.

This jurisprudential transformation—changing the worthier title doctrine from an inflexible rule of law into a rule of construction that yields to an expression of contrary intention—is strikingly unusual and merits a brief discussion. The transformation was the brainchild of Benjamin Cardozo, who announced it in 1919 in the New York case of *Doctor v. Hughes*, 225 N.Y. 305, 122 N.E. 221 (1919), which became an important precedent. The case involved a conveyance of real property to a trustee, to pay the grantor an annuity of $1,500 for life, and upon his death the corpus of the trust was to go to the grantor's "heirs at law." During the grantor's lifetime, creditors of his daughter sought to reach her interest in the trust, arguing that she (as one of the heirs-apparent) had a property interest in the trust. Judge Cardozo rejected their claim on the ground that the grantor's purported gift to his heirs at law amounted to a reversion in himself, and so his daughter had nothing her creditors could attach. This result could have been reached by applying the doctrine of worthier title as a rule of law. But Judge Cardozo was disinclined to decide the case on such a traditional ground. Noting that the doctrine had been abolished in England, Judge Cardozo wrote:

> We do not say that the ancient rule survives as an absolute prohibition limiting the power of a grantor.... But at least the ancient rule survives to this extent: That, to transform into a remainder what would ordinarily be a reversion, the intention [of the grantor] ... must be clearly expressed.

From this time forward, the courts in New York and many other states viewed the inter vivos branch of the worthier title doctrine as a rule of construction.

Thirty years after *Doctor v. Hughes*, a second important decision was issued by New York's highest court: *In re Burchell's Estate*, 87 N.E.2d 293 (N.Y. 1949). In that case, Judge Bromley lowered the level of evidence needed to overcome the doctrine as a rule of construction. He wrote:

> While we have not yet adopted a rule, either by statute or judicial construction, under which language limiting an interest to heirs is unequi-vocally given its full effect, the presumption which exists from

the use of the common-law doctrine as a rule of construction has lost much of its force since *Doctor v. Hughes*. Evidence of intent need not be overwhelming in order to allow the remainder to stand. Whether the rule should be abrogated completely is a matter for the Legislature.

Both of these decisions deserve severe criticism. Shifting a rule of law to a rule of construction, as Judge Cardozo did in *Doctor v. Hughes*, is not a natural evolutionary step in legal development. Rules of law and rules of construction are based on entirely different premises. Rules of law are intent-defeating; rules of construction are intent-effectuating. Defeating intention is only justified to vindicate goals of sound social policy. When the policy reasons that underlie a rule of law disappear, as they have with respect to the worthier title doctrine, the proper course is for the legislature to repeal the rule (as the English legislature did in 1833) or for the courts to abrogate it. Judge Bromley's attempt to weaken the doctrine by lowering the level of evidence needed to overcome it was unwise. Weak presumptions resolve fewer cases, thus increasing the need for litigation. This is precisely what happened in New York. As Professor Richard Powell observed, "no case involving a substantial sum could fairly be regarded as closed until its language and circumstances had been passed upon" by New York's highest court. Richard R. Powell, Cases on Future Interests 88 (3d ed. 1961).

In 1966, the New York legislature overturned the *Doctor* decision by abolishing the doctrine of worthier title even as a rule of construction. Nevertheless, there are a few states, in addition to the previously mentioned Washington, where the inter vivos branch remains alive as a rule of construction. There are also jurisdictions where one can find cases suggesting that the inter vivos branch may still exist as a rule of law. See, e.g., *Randall v. Marble*, 69 Me. 310 (1879).

In states where it exists, the doctrine of worthier title can cause unexpected estate tax consequences by causing some or all of the future interest's value to be included in the grantor's gross estate. See Internal Revenue Code §§ 2033, 2037. The doctrine has also caused problems with trusts drafted to provide at the settlor's death for payment of Medicaid expenses followed by distribution of any remaining assets to the settlor's heirs.

Like the destructibility rule and the Rule in Shelley's Case, the doctrine of worthier title might be viewed as an instrument of social policy, promoting alienability by untying the fetters purportedly imposed on the property by the grantor's original disposition. If the original conveyance was of a legal interest in land, the doctrine enables the grantor subsequently to transfer a fee simple absolute. If the original conveyance was in an irrevocable trust, the doctrine enables the grantor to join with the other beneficiaries in agreeing to the trust's early termination, thereby permitting the property to be transferred free of trust in fee simple absolute.

Nevertheless, the doctrine of worthier title is a poor instrument of policy. It operates in a very narrow range, and its benefits are dwarfed in comparison to the cost of litigation to determine whether the doctrine as a rule of construction has been overridden by the intention of a particular grantor. The court in *Hatch v. Riggs National Bank*, 361 F.2d 559 (D.C. Cir. 1966), persuasively explained why the doctrine should not remain even as a rule of construction:

> We see no reason to plunge the District of Columbia into the ranks of those jurisdictions bogged in the morass of exploring, under the modern doctrine of

worthier title, 'the almost ephemeral qualities which go to prove the necessary intent.' The alleged benefit of effectuating intent must be balanced against the resulting volume of litigation and the diversity and difficulty of decision.

Both the National Conference of Commissioners on Uniform State Laws and the American Law Institute share this view. The Uniform Probate Code provides in § 2-710:

The doctrine of worthier title is abolished as a rule of law and as a rule of construction. Language in a governing instrument describing the beneficiaries of a disposition as the transferor's "heirs," "heirs at law," "next of kin," "distributees," "relatives," or "family," or language of similar import, does not create or presumptively create a reversionary interest in the transferor.

The Restatement 3d of Property likewise rejects the doctrine as a rule of law and as a rule of construction. See Restatement 3d of Property § 16.3. The doctrine does not represent the intentions of the typical transferor, nor can it be justified on grounds of social policy.

§ 6.4 Summary Comparison of the Basic Requirements of the Destructibility Rule, the Rule in Shelley's Case, and the Doctrine of Worthier Title

A table comparing the three feudally-based rules should provide a helpful summary.

Destructibility Rule	*Rule in Shelley's Case*	*Inter Vivos Worthier Title*
A legal contingent remainder in land is destroyed if it has not vested by the time of the termination of the preceding freehold estate	A remainder in land that is purportedly created in the life tenant's heirs or the heirs of the life tenant's body, and that is of the same quality as that of the life estate, is held by the life tenant	When a transferor, by an inter vivos conveyance, purports to create a future interest in the transferor's own heirs, the transferor is presumed to intend to retain a reversionary interest
Feudal basis: livery of seisin	Feudal basis: forcing land to pass by descent rather than by purchase	Feudal basis: forcing land to pass by descent rather than by purchase
Rule of law	Rule of law	Originally rule of law Transformed into rule of construction by judicial interpretation

Destructibility Rule	*Rule in Shelley's Case*	*Inter Vivos Worthier Title*
Merger is one way of causing destructibility; merger, if it takes place, precedes the application of the rule	Merger, if it takes place and it usually does, applies after the operation of the rule, not before	Merger is not relevant
Inter vivos and testamentary transfers	Inter vivos and testamentary transfers	Inter vivos transfers
Only to land	Only to land	Land and personalty
Applicable only to remainders	Only to remainders	Remainders and executory interests
Applicable only to legal contingent remainders	Applicable to legal and equitable remainders, but the remainder and the preceding estate must be of the same quality	No similar requirements; applicable to equitable as well as legal future interests; can be of different quality from prior estate

§ 6.5   Concluding Observations

For the states that have not yet abolished these three rules, we hope that their courts or legislatures will do so promptly. See Thomas P. Gallanis, The Future of Future Interests, 60 Wash. & Lee L. Rev. 513 (2003) (proposing these and other reforms).

The rules discussed in this chapter are obsolete and should disappear from the law, remaining only the province of the historian.[10]

---

[10]Perhaps also the law student. Notwithstanding Parliament's abolition of the Rule in Shelley's Case in 1925, Professor Brian Simpson was still required to learn the rule as an Oxford undergraduate in 1952, "since otherwise, it was argued with perverse but compelling logic, we could not understand what precisely had been abolished." A.W.B. Simpson, Leading Cases in the Common Law 41 (1995).

EXERCISES ON PART I

1. Under the traditional system of classification and the simplified system of classification in the Restatement 3d of Property, classify the present and future interests created in the following transfers:

a. *G* transferred land "to *A* for the life of *B*."

b. *G* transferred land "to *A* for 10 years, then to *B*."

c. *G* transferred land "to *A* for 10 years, then to *B* if *B* is then living."

d. *G* transferred land "to *A* for life, then to *B* if *B* survives *A*, but if not, to *C*."

e. *G* transferred land "to *A* for life, then to *B* if *B* survives *A*, but if not, to *C* if *C* survives *A*."

f. *G* transferred land "to *A* for life, then to *B*, but if *B* fails to survive *A*, to *C*." Do the classifications change if *B* dies before *A*?

g. *G* transferred land "to *A* and his heirs as long as they deliver an orchid on January 1 of each year to me or my successors, otherwise to *B*."

2. Do any of the following interests violate the common-law Rule Against Perpetuities? If an interest is valid, identify the validating life.

a. *G* transferred land "to *A* for life, then to *A*'s children who reach age 30." *G* was survived by *A* and *A*'s daughter, *D*. At *G*'s death, *D* was 31.

b. *G* transferred land "to *A* for life, then to the first child of *A* who reaches age 30." *G* was survived by *A* and *A*'s daughter, *D*. At *G*'s death, *D* was 3.

c. *G* devised land "to *A* for 25 years, then to my heirs at law."

d. *G* transferred land "to *A* for life, then for life to such of *A*'s children as reach age 30, then to *B*." When does *B*'s remainder vest in possession?

3. Analyze the following disposition under the Rule Against Perpetuities as reformulated in the Restatement 3d of Property: *G* transferred property to *T* in trust, directing *T* to distribute the income at *T*'s discretion among *G*'s descendants from time to time living. If at any time *G* no longer has any living descendants, the corpus of the trust is to be paid to X Charity.

PART II

MARITAL ESTATES

CHAPTER 7

MARITAL ESTATES
AT COMMON LAW

The term *marital estates* refers to interests in property that arise as a result of marriage. There were three marital estates at common law: (1) the life estate by and during coverture; (2) dower; and (3) curtesy.

§ 7.1   Life Estate By and During Coverture

The *life estate by and during coverture* was the interest held by a married man in his wife's land as of the date of their marriage. The interest gave the husband the right to possess and administer the land. He could also unilaterally lease or alienate the land for the duration of the marriage, though not after. (An attempt by the husband to convey the land in fee actually conveyed only his marital interest. To convey the fee, the husband and wife would have to act together.) Any rents and profits received from the land during the marriage belonged to the husband absolutely.

The idea behind coverture was that a legal unity existed between husband and wife, making them one person in the eyes of the law. In the words of Sir William Blackstone: "[T]he very being or legal existence of the woman is suspended during the marriage, or at least is incorporated and consolidated into that of the husband." 1 Bl. Com. 430 (1765).

Coverture lasted only during the marriage; the husband's death or the spouses' divorce ended the marital unity, at which point the surviving or former wife regained the power to administer and control her own property.

§ 7.2 Dower

Dower was an interest arising in a surviving wife as of the date of her husband's death. The interest was a life estate in one third of the inheritable land held at any time during the marriage by the husband in fee simple or fee tail.

The principal purpose of dower was to provide support for the surviving widow. It may also have represented a recognition of the wife's contributions to the family estate, and perhaps in addition a partial return of the dowry paid on behalf of the bride. See Thompson on Real Property § 21.02(a). We shall see support and contribution as important rationales for the modern elective share, discussed in the next chapter.

During the husband's life, the wife's right to dower was said to be *inchoate*, but it was still a real right in the following sense: the right to dower could not be defeated by an inter vivos conveyance by the husband to a third party, even to a bona fide purchaser for value. The third party would receive the land subject to the wife's right to dower. (The only exception to this rule occurred if the wife had joined in the conveyance or had otherwise relinquished her right to dower in that land.)

Upon the husband's death, the right to dower became *consummate* if they remained married at his death and the wife survived him. Just as the husband could not by inter vivos conveyance defeat the wife's right to dower, so too could he not defeat the right by will.

An interesting question arose whether the wife could receive both the land devised to her by her husband's will and the land that was hers for life by dower. The rule developed that the wife could take both, unless the will clearly expressed that its provision for the wife was in lieu of dower, in which event the wife would be required to choose. A clear expression of this principle appears in *Birmingham v. Kirwan*, 2 Sch. & Lefr. 444 (Irish Ch. 1805):

> The general rule is, that a person cannot accept and reject the same instrument.... The principle, then, that the wife cannot have both dower and what is given in lieu of dower, being acknowledged ... the only question in such cases must be, whether the provision alleged to have been given in satisfaction of dower was so given, or not....

> As the right to dower is in itself a clear legal right, an intent to exclude that right, by voluntary gift, must be demonstrated either by express words, or by clear and manifest implication. If there was anything ambiguous or doubtful, if the court cannot say that it was clearly the intention to exclude, then the averment that the gift was made in lieu of dower cannot be supported.... [T]he result of all the cases of implied intention seems to

be, that the instrument must contain some provision, inconsistent with the assertion of the right to demand [the dower interest].

§ 7.3   Curtesy

Curtesy was an interest arising in a surviving husband as of the date of his wife's death. The interest was a life estate in all inheritable land held at any time during the marriage by the wife in fee simple or fee tail, or in which the wife had an equitable estate in fee (meaning that the land was held in trust by someone else for the wife's benefit).

Unlike dower, curtesy had an additional requirement: the husband and wife must have had a child born alive during the marriage capable of inheriting the land from its mother.[1]

Upon the child's birth, the husband held an *estate by the curtesy initiate* (akin to the wife's inchoate

---

[1] Thompson on Real Property § 21.03(c) gives the following example: "[T]he instrument giving the estate to the wife may be so worded as to make the issue of the wife purchasers instead of heirs, so far as the [given] estate is concerned. If so, the husband will not have an estate by curtesy."

dower). Upon the wife's death, the husband held an *estate by the curtesy consummate* if they remained married at her death and he survived her. It did not matter whether or not the child survived her.

The purpose of curtesy was not (as one might think) to aid in supporting the marital children. Rather, the purpose seems to have been to maintain the bond between the wife's feudal lord and the husband—a bond created when the husband received his life estate by and during coverture. See Thompson on Real Property § 21.03(b); S.F.C. Milsom, A Natural History of the Common Law 60-61 (2003).

§ 7.4 The Common-Law Marital Estates Today

The *life estate by and during coverture* has been abolished. Women today administer their own property whether or not they are married.

The estates of *dower and curtesy* have been largely abolished. Only a small number of states retain either of these interests.

In place of dower and curtesy, American states provide three layers of protection for a surviving spouse: (1) *statutes of intestate succession*, known formally as *statutes of descent and distribution*, giving the surviving spouse a share of the decedent spouse's intestate estate, (2) statutes authorizing the surviving spouse to take an *elective share* or *forced share* of the decedent spouse's property, and (3) in some states, statutes protecting *omitted spouses* from unrevised premarital wills. There are also states with regimes of *community property*, a concept derived from continental Europe, in which spouses share the assets acquired during marriage. We consider each of these modern protections in the next chapter.

CHAPTER 8

MODERN PROTECTIONS FOR THE SURVIVING SPOUSE

§ 8.1 Introduction

Most jurisdictions in the United States follow the *separate property (or title-based)* system of property ownership that emerged after the elimination of coverture from the common law. Under this system, the husband and wife are separate owners of assets that each person acquires, whether before or during the marriage—except, of course, for items the spouses have agreed to hold jointly. (On concurrent ownership, see Part III.)

One danger of the separate property system is that when the first spouse dies, the surviving spouse may be left penniless. This danger was prevented at common law by the estates of dower and curtesy. In place of the marital estates, most common-law jurisdictions provide two layers of statutory protection for a surviving spouse: (1) statutes of intestate succession, known formally as statutes of descent and distribution, giving the surviving spouse a share of the decedent spouse's intestate estate; and (2) statutes authorizing the surviving spouse to take an elective share of the decedent spouse's property. Some common-law jurisdictions also provide a third layer: protection against inadvertent omission from a premarital will.

§ 8.2   Statutes of Descent and Distribution

A person dying without a valid will has died *intestate*. (When the will does not dispose of all of the decedent's probate property, typically because the will was badly drafted, it is said that the person died *partially intestate*.)

Whether a person dies partially or fully intestate, intestate property is distributed in accordance with intestate succession statutes, known as *statutes of descent and distribution*. This term requires a historical explanation. American statutes on intestate succession are derived from two sources: the common-law canons of descent, which determined inheritance of land; and the English

Statute of Distribution 1670, which governed succession to personal property. Modern American statutes cover both land and personalty and are called statutes of descent and distribution.

All American statutes of descent and distribution give some share of the decedent's intestate property to his or her surviving spouse. (The term "surviving spouse" indicates that the marriage existed at the decedent's death and that the spouse survived the decedent.)

The traditional approach under American law was to give the surviving spouse a fixed fraction of the decedent's intestate estate, commonly one third or one half, fractions derived from common-law dower and the English Statute of Distribution. The fractions might be larger if the decedent had no surviving descendants. Writing in 1953, Professor Thomas Atkinson described the "typical American position" as giving "the spouse half the estate if issue survives; the first $5000 and half the remainder if there is no issue, and parents or their issue survive; the entire estate in other cases." Thomas E. Atkinson, Handbook of the Law of Wills 63 (2d ed. 1953).

A recent trend in American law has been to increase even further the intestate share of the surviving spouse. See Restatement 3d of Property § 2.2. At the forefront of this trend is the Uniform Probate Code, which provides in § 2-102 that the surviving spouse should receive the entire intestate estate even in the presence of surviving descendants if two conditions are met. The first condition is that the decedent's descendants must also be the descendants of the surviving spouse. The second is that the surviving spouse must have no descendants who are not the decedent's descendants. See UPC § 2-102(1)(B).

Example 8.1: G died intestate, survived by his spouse, S, and their two children, X and Y.

Under a statute of the type described by Professor Atkinson, S inherits one half of G's estate. X and Y share the other half equally.

Under the Uniform Probate Code, S inherits G's entire estate.

The move to have the spouse inherit the entire estate despite the presence of children is aligned with statutory reforms throughout the United States, Canada, and Europe. Professor Mary Ann Glendon calls this trend the "shrinking circle of heirs" phenomenon. Mary Ann Glendon, The Transformation of Family Law 238 (1989). By this she means that, over time, "the position of the surviving spouse has steadily improved everywhere at the expense of the decedent's blood relatives."

What explains this phenomenon? The answer is that the aim of intestacy law is to mirror what most decedents would wish if they had thought about it (and had taken the time to execute wills). Marriage increasingly is viewed as the most important family relationship, and decedents accordingly want the bulk if not all of their property to pass to the surviving spouse.

This emphasis on the spouse might appear to prejudice the decedent's children. But UPC § 2-102 is based on the insight that the children are not truly losing. The surviving spouse in fact occupies two roles—one as the decedent's primary beneficiary and one as a conduit through whom to benefit the couple's children.

The theory becomes problematic, of course, when some of the children are not joint. If some of the decedent's descendants are not descendants of the surviving spouse, or vice versa, the likelihood decreases that the spouse will serve as a proper conduit. The UPC responds to this problem by awarding the spouse less than the entire intestate estate in such circumstances. See § 2-102(3), (4).

Example 8.2: (1) G died intestate, survived by his spouse, *S*, and his child, *X*, who is not a child of *S*.

(2) G died intestate, survived by his spouse, *S*, their joint child, *Y*, and *S*'s child, *Z*, who is not a child of *G*.

In both Variations, the Uniform Probate Code awards *S* less than the entire estate. *S* receives the first $150,000 plus one half of the balance of the estate in Variation (1), the first $225,000 plus one half of the estate in Variation (2). See UPC § 2-103(3), (4).

§ 8.3   The Elective Share

Most decedents who execute wills and other estate planning documents provide well for their surviving spouses. Some decedents, however, intentionally attempt to disinherit their surviving spouses, or to provide for them only minimally. This is not permitted under modern law.

All but one of the separate-property states[1] have

---

[1]Georgia is the only separate-property state lacking an elective share statute. For a discussion of the reasons for Georgia's position, including its unusual "year's support" practice, and an argument that elective share statutes are generally unnecessary, see Verner F. Chaffin, A Reappraisal

decided that disinheritance of the surviving spouse at death is one of the few instances in which the decedent's testamentary freedom with respect to his or her title-based ownership interests must be curtailed. No matter what the decedent's intent, the separate-property states recognize that the surviving spouse has a claim to a portion of the decedent's estate. These statutes provide the spouse a so-called *forced share*. Because the forced share is expressed as an option that the survivor can elect or let lapse during the administration of the decedent's estate, the better and more descriptive term is an *elective share*.

Under traditional elective share law, the surviving spouse is entitled to a one-third share of the decedent's probate estate. The term "probate estate" refers to assets that pass under the direction of the decedent's will or, in the absence of an effective will, in accordance with the provisions of the statute of descent and distribution. The term does not include assets owned or owned in substance by the decedent that pass outside the

of the Wealth Transmission Process: The Surviving Spouse, Year's Support and Intestate Succession, 10 Ga. L. Rev. 447 (1976). For an opposing view, see Note, Preventing Spousal Disinheritance in Georgia, 19 Ga. L. Rev. 427 (1985).

probate court's jurisdiction, such as pension or life-insurance proceeds distributed according to a beneficiary designation on file with the decedent's employer or life insurer, assets held in a revocable trust distributed according to the trust's terms, or assets (such as a joint bank account) held by the decedent and another person as joint owners with an automatic right of survivorship.

The traditional law of the elective share provides inadequate protection for the surviving spouse, in two respects. First, the limitation to the probate estate enables the decedent to evade the surviving spouse's entitlement; the decedent can readily place his or her wealth in vehicles such as revocable trusts and joint accounts that pass property outside probate.[2] Second, the fixed fraction (usually one third) is not responsive to the length of the marriage, which is the period of time during which the couple will have accumulated

---

[2] Courts occasionally hold such transfers fraudulent or illusory, hence still subject to the elective share. See *Newman v. Dore*, 275 N.Y. 371, 9 N.E.2d 966 (1937); *Sullivan v. Burkin*, 390 Mass. 864, 460 N.E.2d 572 (1984). The better remedy is a statute, such as the Uniform Probate Code, expressly including nonprobate transfers within the elective share.

assets together; it is on these assets that the surviving spouse has a moral claim that should be actualized in law. For discussion, see Restatement 3d of Property §§ 9.1, 9.2.

Example 8.3: (1) G and *S* were married for 1 year. Then *G* died with a will leaving "all my property to X Charity." *G*'s probate estate was worth $3 million.

(2) G and *S* were married for 50 years, then *G* died with a will leaving "all my property to X Charity." *G*'s probate estate was worth $3,000, but *G* also owned an insurance policy worth $3 million naming his mistress, *M*, as the beneficiary.

Under the traditional elective share, *S* is entitled to $1 million in Variation (1) and $1,000 in Variation (2).

Newer elective share statutes, such as the Uniform Probate Code, address both of these deficiencies. First, the UPC reaches beyond the probate estate to a broad range of assets owned or owned in substance by the decedent, including assets passing outside probate. See UPC § 2-205. This broad range of assets is called the "augmented estate." UPC § 2-203(a). Second, the surviving spouse's entitlement is linked to the length of the marriage. Put differently: the UPC entitles the surviving spouse to 50 percent of the marital property portion of the augmented estate. A sliding percentage based on the length of the marriage is used to determine the marital property portion. For example, in a marriage lasting 15 years or more, the marital property portion is 100 percent, meaning that the surviving spouse is entitled to one-half of 100 percent—50 percent—of the augmented estate. To take another example, in a marriage lasting at least one year but less than two years, the marital property portion is 6 percent, meaning that the surviving spouse is entitled to one-half of 6 percent—3 percent—of the augmented estate. See UPC §§ 2-202(a), 2-203(b).[3]

§ 8.4 Inadvertent Omission from Premarital Will

Nearly all American jurisdictions have statutes, called "pretermitted heir" statutes, that grant the decedent's children a measure of protection from being inadvertently disinherited. The statutes typically apply when the decedent's will was

---

[3]The UPC also provides for a supplemental share, where needed, to bring the spouse's assets plus the spouse's elective share to $75,000. See UPC § 2-202(b).

executed before the child was born or adopted.

Similar protection for the surviving spouse is uncommon, although some states provide it. See Restatement 3d of Property § 9.5. The protection is particularly evident in those states adopting § 2-301 of the Uniform Probate Code. The section provides that if the decedent executed the will before the marriage, the surviving spouse is entitled to receive a share of the decedent's probate estate, unless (1) it appears that the will was made in contemplation of the marriage, (2) the will expresses the intention to omit the future spouse, or (3) the decedent provided for the spouse outside the will and there is evidence that such provision was intended to be in lieu of a share of the will.

If this rule entitles the spouse to a share, there is still the matter of computing the share. The UPC section in its current form provides that the share is to be the amount the spouse would have received if the decedent had died intestate as to that portion of the estate not devised to a descendant of the decedent (but not of the surviving spouse) born before the marriage, or passing to such a person's descendants under an antilapse statute. This may seem a bit complicated, but it is illustrated in the following examples.

Example 8.4: G and *S-1* were married for thirty years. After *S-1* died, G married *S-2*. G died with a will executed while *S-1* was alive, giving "all my property to *S-1*, if *S-1* survives me, and if not, to X Charity."

In most non-UPC jurisdictions, G's property passes to X Charity, except for whatever *S-2* may claim as an elective share.

Under UPC § 2-301, *S-2* is entitled to the property *S-2* would have received if G had died intestate as to the portion of G's estate not passing to a descendant of G. On these facts, nothing is passing to such a descendant, so *S-2* is entitled to G's entire estate.

Example 8.5: G and *S-1* were married for thirty years and had a child, *C*. After *S-1* died, G married *S-2*. G died with a will executed while *S-1* was alive, giving "all my property to *S-1*, if *S-1* survives me, and if not, to *C* if *C* survives me, and if not, to X Charity." G was survived by *S-2* and *C*.

In most non-UPC jurisdictions and also under the UPC, G's estate passes to *C*, except for whatever *S-2* may claim as an elective share.

The animating principle behind the Uniform

Probate Code's protection of the omitted spouse—and its withdrawal of the protection in certain circumstances, particularly where there are devises to children or descendants from a prior relationship—is that these results are the ones the testator would want if he or she had taken the trouble to execute a new will.

§ 8.5   Community Property

So far, we have been speaking of the separate property or title-based system of property ownership, which is derived from English common law and is today followed by most jurisdictions in the United States. There is an alternative. The system known as *community property* developed in continental Europe and was transplanted to the new world by French and Spanish settlers. In a community property system, the husband and wife own all assets acquired by either of them during the marriage in equal undivided shares. The particular community property model appearing in this country is derived from the *community of acquests* concept of the Spanish legal system, under which each spouse owns a half interest in the earnings of the other acquired during the marriage, in effect as a tenant in common (on this term, see § 9.2);[4] property acquired prior to the marriage and property acquired during the marriage by gift or inheritance are not counted in the community, and so remain separate property. The other community property model, called universal community, has not appeared in this country. In universal community systems, each spouse owns a half interest in all the property of the other, regardless of the property's source or time of acquisition.

Nine   states   (Arizona,   California,   Idaho, Louisiana,   Nevada,   New   Mexico,   Texas,

[4]Because both spouses own community property, problems arise concerning the management of community assets. Community property states have statutes prescribing who has power to manage and deal with the assets. These statutes vary considerably, but some generalizations are possible. In Texas, the wife has sole management power over her earnings that are kept separate, and the husband has sole management power over his. In California and several other community property states, either spouse has power, acting alone, to manage community assets. Both spouses, however, ordinarily are required to join in transfers or mortgages of community real property. If one spouse makes a gift of community property to a third party, the non-donor spouse may set it aside entirely or in excess of a stated amount. See J. Thomas Oldham, Management of the Community Estate During an Intact Marriage, 56 L. & Contemp. Prob. 99 (1993).

Washington, and Wisconsin[5]) are community property states. Alaska is an optional community property state, meaning that married persons may choose to classify some or all of their assets as community property.[6]

Interest in community property has been growing, thanks to an emerging consensus in favor of economic equalization between husbands and wives. The idea that both marital partners should share equally acquests from the economic activity

[5]Wisconsin's enactment of the Model Marital Property Act made it a community property state. The Wisconsin legislature, however, modified the MMPA in several respects. See Howard S. Erlanger & June M. Weisberger, From Common Law Property to Community Property: Wisconsin's Marital Property Act Four Years Later, 1990 Wis. L. Rev. 769 (1990).

[6]For discussion, see Jonathan G. Blattmachr, Howard M. Zaritsky & Mark L. Ascher, Tax Planning with Consensual Community Property: Alaska's New Community Property Law, 33 Real Prop., Prob. & Tr. J. 615 (1999). The Alaska Community Property Act, effective May 23, 1998, also permits residents and non-residents to establish community property trusts, holding specific assets as community property. See Jonathan G. Blattmachr & Howard M. Zaritsky, Alaska Consensual Community Property Law and Property Trust, Tr. & Est. 65 (Nov. 1998).

of either led to the promulgation in 1983 of the Uniform Marital Property Act, now called the Model Marital Property Act. The MMPA adopts a version of the community of acquests, although the terminology is different: community property is called "marital property" and separate property is called "individual property." Under the MMPA, as under community property, the property interest that each spouse acquires in all the assets acquired by the economic activities of either during the marriage is a present, vested ownership right that does not depend on survival of the other spouse.[7]

---

[7] Under community property systems and the MMPA, the couple's property must be classified upon the first spouse's death, and this in turn sometimes requires tracing the property to its source. To help resolve disputes, these systems recognize a presumption that all property is community or marital property. The spouse alleging that an item is separate or individual property must be able to prove it, and this can be a difficult task as assets over time in a marriage are commingled, invested, reinvested, exchanged, and consumed. To resolve classification problems, courts have developed numerous rules applicable to particular types of transactions.

Problems also arise because a couple has moved from a separate property state to a community property state, or the reverse. The basic principle is that the law of the state where the couple was domiciled at the time an asset was acquired controls ownership of the asset.

Detailed consideration of these questions is beyond the

A unique feature of community property regimes is that the surviving spouse is not seen as needing an elective share to protect against disinheritance. The survivor already owns a half interest in the fruits of the marriage. The survivor's contribution having been rewarded, the decedent can be allowed unfettered power of disposition over his or her separate property and his or her portion of the community property.[8]

Example 8.6: G and S, married for fifty years, hold all their assets as community property. G died with a will leaving "all my property to X Charity."

G is entitled to dispose of one half of the community. S retains one half. No elective share is needed to prevent disinheritance.

scope of this *Nutshell*.

[8]In practice, decedents often wish to benefit their surviving spouses. Some states permit spouses to create "community property with right of survivorship," which passes automatically to the survivor as if in joint tenancy. See, e.g., Ariz. Stat. § 33-431; Cal. Civ. Code § 682.1; Idaho Code § 15-6-401; Nev. Stat. § 111.064; Tex. Est. Code § 112.051.

PART III

CONCURRENT ESTATES

CHAPTER 9

CONCURRENT ESTATES

§ 9.1 Introduction

Anglo-American law permits multiple persons to hold the same interests in the same property. Because these interests are held concurrently, rather than successively, they are known as *concurrent estates*.

Consider the following example.

Example 9.1: G transferred land "to *A* and *B* and their heirs."[1]

---

[1]In most of the remaining examples in this chapter, the words of limitation "and their heirs" will be omitted. Under

A and *B* each hold a fee simple absolute. Their interests are concurrent, not successive.

Three concurrent estates exist today: (1) joint tenancy, (2) tenancy in common, and (3) tenancy by the entirety. The fourth—tenancy in coparcenary—no longer exists.

§ 9.2   The Tenancies Defined

Joint tenancy[2] is a concurrent estate held by multiple persons who share what are traditionally called the *four unities*:

(1) *unity of time*: the persons receive their interests in the property at the same moment;

(2) *unity of title*: the persons receive their interests from the same source, meaning the same deed or will;

(3) *unity of interest*: the persons receive the same type of interest, e.g., a fee simple absolute or a life estate; and

modern law, these words are unnecessary to create interests in fee simple absolute. (Recall § 2.3.)

[2]This material refers primarily to joint tenancies in land. On the joint bank account, see § 9.8.

(4) *unity of possession*: each person has the same right to possess the property.

One important feature of a joint tenancy is that the joint tenants have a *right of survivorship*. When one joint tenant dies, his or her interest in the property automatically passes to the other joint tenants. The interest does not pass to the decedent's devisees or heirs.

Example 9.2: G transferred land "to *A* and *B* as joint tenants and not as tenants in common." Later, *A* died with a will devising "all my property to my niece, *N*." *A*'s heir at law was his son, *S*. *A* was survived by *B*, *N*, and *S*.

A's interest in the land passes automatically at *A*'s death to *B*. It does not pass to *N* or *S*.

Joint tenancies are recognized in most American jurisdictions, but not all. Some states have abolished the joint tenancy. For example, Alaska has abolished joint tenancies in land, and Oregon has re-labeled the joint tenancy as "tenancy in common in the life estate with cross-contingent remainders in the fee simple." See Alaska Stat. § 34.15.130; Or. Rev. Stat. § 93.180. Some other states recognize the joint tenancy but not its right of survivorship. See, e.g., Ark. Code § 28-8-101; Fla. Stat. § 689.15; Tenn. Code § 66-1-107.

Tenancy in common is a concurrent estate requiring only one unity: the *unity of possession*, meaning that each tenant in common has the same right to possess the property. Tenancy in common does not have the survivorship feature of joint tenancy. When one tenant in common dies, his or her interest passes to his or her devisees or heirs, not to the other tenants in common.

> *Example 9.3:* G transferred land "to A and B as tenants in common." Later, A died with a will devising "all my property to my niece, N." A's heir at law was his son, S. A was survived by B, N, and S.
>
> A's interest in the land passes by will to N. There is no right of survivorship between A and B.

On the current preference for tenancy in common over joint tenancy, see § 9.3 below.

Tenancy by the entirety is a special form of joint tenancy existing only between husband and wife. At common law, it was said that tenancy by the entirety required five unities: the four unities of joint tenancy plus a fifth unity—*unity of person*. (Recall the common law view that husband and wife were one person; see § 7.1.) Like joint tenancy, tenancy by the entirety includes an automatic right of survivorship.

> *Example 9.4:* G transferred land "to A and B, husband and wife, as tenants by the entirety." Later, A died with a will devising "all my property to my niece, N." A's heirs at law were his wife, B, and his son, S. A was survived by B, N, and S.
>
> A's interest in the land passes automatically at A's death to B. It does not pass to N or S.

Today, a majority of American jurisdictions have abolished the tenancy by the entirety; these states recognize only the joint tenancy and the tenancy in common.

Tenancy in coparcenary was the concurrent estate created at common law in England when land was inherited by two or more persons (in contrast to the typical practice, primogeniture, which involved inheritance by one heir, the eldest male).

> *Example 9.5:* G transferred land "to A and his heirs." Later, A died without a will, survived by his daughters, X and Y, who were his heirs.
>
> A's interest in the land passes by descent to X and Y as coparceners.

American jurisdictions never recognized this tenancy. Instead, the concurrent estates created when a decedent dies intestate survived by multiple heirs are generally tenancies in common. This is true even though some statutes use the terminology of the tenancy in coparcenary. See Thompson on Real Property §§ 31.01, 35.08.

§ 9.3   The Creation of Concurrent Estates

At common law, joint tenancy was the preferred form of concurrent ownership. A transfer of property by deed or will to "*A* and *B* and their heirs" created a joint tenancy.[3]

Modern statutes and judicial decisions, however, prefer the tenancy in common. In the majority of states, the law now presumes that a transfer to multiple persons creates a tenancy in common unless the transferor manifests an intention to create a joint tenancy.[4]

---

[3]Unless *A* and *B* were husband and wife, in which case the transfer created a tenancy by the entirety.

[4]Among the states recognizing the tenancy by the entirety, there is a split of authority on whether a transfer to spouses is presumed to create a tenancy by the entirety, on the one hand, or a tenancy in common or joint tenancy, on the other. There is also a split of authority on the effect of a transfer to

The rationale for the modern approach seems to be that the recipients of property should not enjoy an automatic right of survivorship unless the transferor has evidenced the intention to create the right. There has been much litigation on whether a particular transferor has or has not provided sufficient evidence of intention. Consider the following example.

Example 9.6: G transferred land "to *A* and *B* jointly."

In states with a presumption in favor of tenancy in common, the lone word "jointly" will typically be insufficient to overcome the presumption; *A* and *B* will take as tenants in common. In a few states, however, the statute creating the presumption expressly allows the presumption to be rebutted by the word "jointly"; in which case, *A* and *B* will take as joint tenants. See Thompson on Real Property § 31.06(d).

Another much litigated question concerns the ability of a transferor to create a joint tenancy by

unmarried persons "as tenants by the entirety." Some jurisdictions treat this as a joint tenancy, others as a tenancy in common.

conveying the property to himself and another. At common law, this did not satisfy the required unities of time and title—each joint tenant must receive the interest from the same document at the same time. Accordingly, the practice developed of using a middleman: G would convey the land to X who would convey it to G and A as joint tenants. In the majority of states, this two-step procedure is no longer necessary; substance prevails over form, and a transferor may convey property to himself and one or more third parties as joint tenants.

Example 9.7: G transferred land "to G and A as joint tenants."

In the majority of states, this transfer suffices to create a joint tenancy. G and A hold as joint tenants, i.e., with an automatic right of survivorship between them.

A similar rule prevails in the states recognizing the tenancy by the entirety: one spouse may convey to both spouses as tenants by the entirety, as in the following example.

Example 9.8: G transferred land "to G and A, husband and wife, as tenants by the entirety."

This transfer is sufficient to create a tenancy by the entirety in most of the states recognizing the tenancy.

§ 9.4   Relations Among Concurrent Tenants

As we have seen in § 9.2, the holders of any concurrent estate enjoy unity of possession, meaning the same right to possess and enjoy the whole property. This means that a cotenant in exclusive possession does not owe rent to the other cotenants.

> *Example 9.9:* G transferred land "to A and B" as tenants in common or as joint tenants (in this example, it makes no difference). A is occupying the land; B lives elsewhere.
>
> A has the right to possess and enjoy the entire land. A does not owe rent to B. Nor, without more, is A's sole occupancy adverse to B for purposes of adverse possession.

Conversely, no cotenant has the right to exclude the other cotenants. Such exclusion would be an ouster, enabling the ousted cotenant to maintain an action to regain possession (and an appropriate share of any profits). Indeed, if the ousted cotenant did not bring an action, he or she could eventually lose title by adverse possession.

It frequently happens that not all cotenants are in possession at any given time. It is worth repeating that this by itself is not an ouster (and would not lead to title by adverse possession), because each cotenant has the right to possess the whole.

When not all cotenants are in possession, questions arise about the rights and obligations of the cotenants in possession with respect to those who are not.

The background rule at common law is that the cotenants in possession may treat the property as their own. There are two important limitations to this rule, however. First, the Statute of Anne 1704, as interpreted by the English judges, required the cotenants in possession to account to the other cotenants for any rents received from a third person.

> *Example 9.10:* G transferred land "to A and B" as cotenants. A occupies the land; B lives elsewhere. A rents a room on the land to X at the rate of $1,000 per month.
>
> B is entitled to $500 per month from A. If A refuses to pay it, B may bring an action of account against A to force payment.

Most American jurisdictions follow this English statute, either by legislation or by declaring it to be part of their common law, and some extend it to other forms of income and profits generated by the cotenant in possession himself.

Example 9.11: G transferred land "to *A* and *B*" as cotenants. *A* occupies the land; *B* lives elsewhere. *A* removed and sold minerals from the land, earning a net profit of $10,000.

In some jurisdictions, the duty to account (rather than the duty to avoid waste, see below) applies to these facts, meaning that *B* is entitled to a pro rata share of the net profits, in this instance $5,000. If *A* refuses to pay it, *B* may bring an action of account to force payment. See, e.g., *White v. Smyth*, 147 Tex. 272, 214 S.W.2d 967 (1948).

Second, the cotenants in possession may not permit or cause the property to suffer permanent damage ("waste"). What constitutes waste varies widely from one jurisdiction to another, and even when damage such as cutting timber or removing minerals is labeled waste, the typical remedy is simply the same as we have already observed for rents and profits: an accounting to the other cotenants for the net profits received. Rarely is the traditional English penalty for waste—treble damages—imposed against cotenants by American courts.

If the cotenants in possession spend money on the property without the consent (express or implied) of the cotenants not in possession, the extent to which the former may require contribution from the latter depends on whether the expenditures were for necessary repairs or for improvements. If for improvements, the widespread rule is that no contribution is required.[5] If for necessary repairs, American jurisdictions are split. Some permit contribution if consent was requested but denied, on the theory that the expenditures were necessary and the withholding of consent was unreasonable; others do not because no consent was obtained.

If a cotenant pays more than his or her share of an obligation imposed by law or by agreement—e.g., taxes or a mortgage—he or she is of course entitled to contribution from the other cotenants.

Example 9.12: G transferred land "to *A* and *B*" as cotenants. *A* occupies the land; *B* lives elsewhere. *A* paid property taxes of $2,000,

---

[5]While the cotenancy exists. In an action for partition (on which see § 9.5), the cotenants in possession can obtain contribution as a part of the final accounting, if the improvements increased the value of the land.

spent $500 mending a leaky roof, and spent $5,000 on fancy landscaping.

A is entitled to contribution from *B* in the amount of $1,000 for the property taxes, and in some jurisdictions (if consent was sought but not obtained) to contribution in the amount of $250 for the roof repair. *A* is not entitled to contribution for the landscaping.[6]

§ 9.5   The Termination of Concurrent Estates

The methods of terminating a concurrent estate vary according to the nature of the estate.

Tenancies in common can be terminated by a *voluntary partition* initiated by all cotenants and effected by an exchange of deeds among them; or if the cotenants cannot agree, any one of them can bring an *action for partition*. Either way, the result of the successful partition is to destroy the unity of possession, subdividing the property into separate parcels each owned by one of the former cotenants. This is called *partition in kind*.

---

[6]Except perhaps in the final accounting accompanying an action for partition, if the landscaping increases the value of the property. See the previous footnote.

Example 9.13: G transferred unimproved land "to *A* and *B* as tenants in common." Later, *A* brought an action for partition.

The result of the partition is that the land is divided into two parcels, one owned by *A*, the other owned by *B*.

If physical division is impractical—e.g., because the property contains indivisible improvements, such as a house—the proper course is *partition by sale* (again, voluntarily or by court action), whereby the property is sold and the proceeds divided among the former cotenants.

Example 9.14: G transferred land containing a single-family home "to *A* and *B* as tenants in common." *A* occupies the home; *B* lives elsewhere. *A* later brings an action for partition.

The result of the action will be partition by sale, with the proceeds divided between *A* and *B*. Note that *A* (or *B*) might be the purchaser at the sale.

Joint tenancies are also subject to partition in kind or by sale. Short of partition, a joint tenancy can be transformed into a tenancy in common by severing the joint tenancy—in other words, by destroying one or more (but not all) of the four unities. This typically results from a conveyance by a joint tenant to a third party. Consider the following example.

Example 9.15: G transferred land "to *A*, *B*, and *C* as joint tenants and not as tenants in common." Later, *A* conveyed her interest in the land to *X*. Still later, *X* died intestate survived by his sole heir, *H*. Then *B* died.

The conveyance from *A* to *X* severs the joint tenancy (and the right of survivorship) between *A* and *B* and between *A* and *C*. After the conveyance, *X* holds the land as a tenant in common with *B* and *C*, who hold as joint tenants with each other. On *X*'s death, *X*'s interest passes to his heir, *H*. Because *B* and *C* hold the land as joint tenants with each other, when *B* dies before *C*, *B*'s one-third interest passes automatically to *C*. *C* and *H* then hold unequal shares as tenants in common.

The cases are divided on whether the conveyance must be to a third party. (Recall the discussion of the middleman in § 9.3.) Some jurisdictions permit a joint tenancy to be severed, hence transformed into a tenancy in common, by a joint tenant transferring his interest to himself. See, e.g., *Riddle v. Harmon*, 102 Cal.App.3d 524 (1980).

Example 9.16: G transferred land "to A and B as joint tenants and not as tenants in common." Later, A transferred his interest in the land "to A as tenant in common."

In some jurisdictions, the transfer is effective to sever the joint tenancy, transforming it into a tenancy in common, hence without a right of survivorship between A and B.

There is also uncertainty about whether actions short of a conveyance will be sufficient to trigger a severance of the joint tenancy. Some cases and authorities state that a mortgage or lease of one joint tenant's interest will be sufficient; others take the opposite view. Am. L. Prop. § 6.2; Thompson on Real Property § 31.08(b).

The *tenancy by the entirety* is subject to partition, but only if both spouses agree. The agreement of both spouses is also generally needed to convey an interest to a third party. Absent partition, a tenancy by the entirety will terminate only on death or divorce. In the latter event, jurisdictions are divided on whether the former spouses—if they continue to hold concurrent estates—are tenants in common or joint tenants.

§ 9.6   Creditors' Rights

An overarching principle governing the rights of creditors in concurrent estates is that the creditor can have no greater rights than the debtor. Hence, the following material is largely an application of the principles discussed in § 9.5.

The creditor of a *tenant in common* can reach only that tenant's share. The other cotenants retain their proportionate shares, which they can transfer to third parties. Partition also remains an option.

> *Example 9.17:* G transferred land "to A, B, and C as tenants in common." A has accumulated substantial debts to X.
>
> X may reach A's share of the land, but not the shares of B and C.

The creditor of a *joint tenant* may (as with tenancy in common) seek partition. Short of partition, the creditor should act promptly to sever the estate, transforming it into a tenancy in common. (This is typically done by the execution of a lien on the property then a judgment sale of the debtor-tenant's interest.) If the creditor fails to act while the debtor-tenant is alive, the creditor will be too late. The right of survivorship will operate at the debtor-tenant's death, leaving nothing within the creditor's reach.

   Example 9.18: G transferred land "to *A*, *B*, and *C* as joint tenants and not as tenants in common." *A* has accumulated large debts to *X*.

   X must act while *A* is alive to sever or partition the tenancy. If the land remains in joint tenancy at *A*'s death, the right of survivorship operates to transfer *A*'s interest to *B* and *C*, with nothing reachable by *X*.

The creditor of one spouse who holds property as a *tenant by the entirety* will generally be unable to reach the property. Most states recognizing the tenancy hold that it may be reached only by a creditor of both spouses. See, e.g., *Sawada v. Endo*, 57 Haw. 608, 561 P.2d 1291 (1977). The U.S. Supreme Court has held, however, that this rule of state law does not apply when the creditor is the federal government: in *United States v. Craft*, 535 U.S. 274 (2002), the Court upheld a federal tax lien imposed when one spouse, but not the other, owed substantial sums to the Internal Revenue Service.

   Example 9.19: G transferred land "to *A* and *B*, husband and wife, as tenants by the entirety." *A* (but not *B*) has accumulated significant debts to *X*.

X cannot reach the land in most states recognizing the tenancy by the entirety, unless *X* is the federal government.

Before *Craft*, the tenancy by the entirety offered a protective shield to married persons by insulating the marital home from creditors. In the words of one case, "the archaic fiction of a tenancy by the entireties is preserved [in modern law] only because it makes it almost impossible for creditors to reach a debtor's family house." *Harris v. Crowder*, 174 W.Va. 83, 322 S.E.2d 854 (1984). The decision in *Craft* represents a noteworthy breach in this protective shield. Whether *Craft* will lead to the further erosion—perhaps even the abolition—of the tenancy by the entirety remains to be seen.

§ 9.7 Rights of the Surviving Spouse

The decedent's proportionate fraction of land held as *tenant in common* is devisable and descendible. Thus, if the decedent dies partially or completely intestate, the surviving spouse will receive an intestate share (see § 8.2). If the decedent's will devises the property to a third party, the surviving spouse will be entitled to an elective share (see § 8.3).

Land held by a decedent and a third party as *joint tenants* is neither devisable nor descendible. Rather, the right of survivorship automatically operates at the decedent's death. Nothing is left for the decedent's spouse to inherit—or, under traditional law, to claim in the elective share. The Uniform Probate Code's elective share, however, takes the opposite approach. The UPC provides that the surviving spouse is entitled to an elective share in "[t]he decedent's fractional interest in property held by the decedent in joint tenancy ... to the extent the fractional interest passed by right of survivorship at the decedent's death to a surviving joint tenant other than the decedent's surviving spouse." UPC § 2-205(1)(B).

> *Example 9.20:* G transferred land "to A and B as joint tenants and not as tenants in common." Later, A died, survived by his spouse, S.
>
> In many non-UPC jurisdictions, the land passes automatically at A's death to B and cannot be reached by S's elective share.
>
> Under the UPC, the land is subject to S's elective share.

Property held by the decedent and the surviving spouse as *tenants by the entirety* passes automatically to the surviving spouse.

§ 9.8   A Footnote on Joint Bank Accounts

Joint bank and other financial organization accounts typically contain a survivorship feature. The balance on hand in the account at the death of a depositor shifts automatically to the surviving joint account holders without going through probate. Except in a very few states, however, the funds in a joint account are not owned in joint tenancy (or tenancy by the entirety, if between spouses). That is to say, a deposit into such an account does not in most states transfer an undivided interest therein to the other account holders. The fact that each account holder can as a matter of practice withdraw the whole of the account masks the true ownership of the funds. The true ownership is that each account holder owns only his or her contributions. See Uniform Probate Code § 6-211. If one co-account holder withdraws an amount in excess of his or her contributions, the other account holders normally have the right to force the excess to be returned.

EXERCISES ON PARTS II AND III

1. *G* transferred land "to *A*, *B*, and *C* as tenants in common." What happens if:

a. *A* transfers his interest to *X*?

b. *A* dies intestate, survived by his sole heir, *H*?

c. *A* dies, survived by his spouse, *S*, and with a will devising "all of my property to X Charity"?

2. *G* transferred land "to *A*, *B*, and *C* as joint tenants and not as tenants in common." What happens if:

a. *A* transfers his interest to *X*?

b. *A* dies, survived by his sole heir, *H*?

c. *A* dies intestate, survived by his spouse, *S*, and with a will devising "all of my property to X-Charity"?

3. *G* transferred land "to *A*, *B*, and *C* as tenants in common with the right of survivorship." What result?

PART IV

POWERS OF APPOINTMENT

CHAPTER 10

A PRIMER ON POWERS

Professor W. Barton Leach described the power of appointment as "the most efficient dispositive device that the ingenuity of Anglo-American lawyers has ever worked out." Powers of Appointment, 24 A.B.A. J. 807 (1938). This device is the subject of the remaining chapters.

§ 10.1   Definitions and Terminology

A *power of appointment* is generally defined as a power to designate a recipient of an ownership interest in, or a power of appointment over, specified property. See Uniform Powers of Appointment Act § 102(13); Restatement 3d of Property § 17.1. An owner, of course, has this authority with respect to his or her property. By creating a power of appointment, the owner confers this authority on someone who is not the property's owner.

The property subject to a power of appointment is called the *appointive property*. The property interest subject to appointment need not be an absolute-ownership interest. In fact, powers of appointment frequently involve appointment of a remainder interest, as in the following example.

Example 10.1: G transferred property in trust, providing for "income to A for life, remainder in corpus to those of A's descendants as A shall by will appoint; in default of appointment, to X Charity."

A subsequently died, leaving a will that exercised her power of appointment in favor of her adult child, B.

The parties connected to a power of appointment are identified by a special terminology. The *donor* is the person who created or reserved the power of appointment—G in the above example. The *powerholder* (in older terminology, the *donee*) is the person upon whom the power of appointment was conferred or in whom the power was reserved—A in the above example.

The *permissible appointees* (in older terminology, the *objects*) are the persons in whose favor the power can be exercised—*A*'s descendants in the above example. The donor determines who are the permissible appointees by expressly designating them in the instrument creating the power. If the donor does not expressly designate permissible appointees, the powerholder is free in almost all states to appoint in favor of anyone in the world, including the powerholder, the powerholder's estate, the creditors of the powerholder, or the creditors of the powerholder's estate.

The *appointee* is the person to whom an appointment has been made—*B* in the above example. The appointment makes the appointee the owner of the appointed property interest.

The *taker in default of appointment* (or simply, *taker in default*) is the person who takes the appointive property to the extent that the power is not effectively exercised—X Charity in the above example. The taker in default has a property interest that is subject to the power of appointment. Upon *A*'s death, X Charity's property interest was divested in favor of the appointee, *B*.

In all cases, there is a donor, a powerholder, and someone in whose favor an appointment can be made. The other parties are not indispensable. The powerholder is under no duty to exercise a power of appointment and, therefore, appointees might not always exist. Also, the donor need not expressly designate takers in default.

§ 10.2   Powers are Personal

A power of appointment is personal to the powerholder. If the powerholder dies without exercising the power, the power expires. The power does not pass to the powerholder's successors in interest. See Uniform Powers of Appointment Act § 202; Restatement 3d of Property § 17.1 cmt. b.

The powerholder can, however, exercise the power to create another power in another powerholder. If a powerholder exercises a power in this way, the powerholder of the first power is the *donor* of the second power, and the powerholder of the second power is an appointee of the first power. See Restatement 3d of Property §§ 17.2 cmt. c, 19.13, 19.14.

§ 10.3   Classification of Powers

Powers of appointment are differentiated in many

ways. Two of the most important distinctions are between presently exercisable and testamentary powers, and between general and nongeneral powers. Both of these distinctions relate to the scope of the powerholder's authority. An extremely important, overarching principle—followed in almost all states—is that the scope of the powerholder's authority is presumptively unlimited. That is, the powerholder's authority as to appointees and the time and manner of appointment is limited only to the extent the donor effectively manifests an intent to impose limits. See Uniform Powers of Appointment Act § 203.

When the terms of a power provide that the powerholder can exercise the power only in the powerholder's will, the power is *testamentary*. When the powerholder can exercise the power either in an inter vivos instrument or in the powerholder's will, the power is *presently exercisable*. (Sometimes the powerholder can exercise a power only in an inter vivos instrument. This type of power is sometimes described as a power exercisable by deed alone, although technically the power can be exercised by any instrument or act that is formally sufficient under applicable law to accomplish an inter vivos transfer.) Testamentary exercises of powers to appoint a remainder are rarely prohibited, but some powers, such as powers to revoke or amend a trust, or to invade the corpus of a trust, are generally thought to be inherently restricted to inter vivos exercises.

A *general* power is one that is exercisable in favor of the powerholder, the powerholder's estate, the powerholder's creditors, or the creditors of the powerholder's estate. A *nongeneral* power is one in which the powerholder, the powerholder's estate, the powerholder's creditors, and the creditors of the powerholder's estate are excluded as permissible appointees.

In accordance with the overarching presumption of unlimited authority, powers are assumed in most jurisdictions to be *general* and *presently exercisable* in the absence of express language indicating otherwise. See Uniform Powers of Appointment Act § 203. An exception is Maryland, which requires express language in order to appoint to the powerholder, the powerholder's estate, or the creditors of either. See *Frank v. Frank*, 253 Md. 413, 253 A.2d 377 (1969).

The classifications are illustrated in the following examples.

Example 10.2: G transferred land "to A for life, remainder to such person or persons as A shall appoint; in default of appointment, remainder to B."

A holds a presently exercisable general power. It is presently exercisable because G did not expressly restrict the exercise of the power either to a will or to an inter vivos instrument. The power is general because G did not forbid A from exercising the power in A's own favor.

Example 10.3: G transferred land "to A for life, remainder to such of A's descendants as A shall by will appoint; in default of appointment, remainder to B."

A holds a nongeneral testamentary power. It is testamentary because G inserted the phrase "by will." Thus any purported inter vivos exercise of the power would be invalid. The power is nongeneral because A is authorized to appoint only among A's own descendants, a group that doesn't include A. (The possibility that one of A's descendants might turn out to be a creditor of A is ignored. See Restatement 3d of Property § 17.3 illus. 2.)

Another way that powers of appointment are differentiated is on the basis of the powerholder's property interest, if any, in the appointive property. There are three categories: collateral powers, powers in gross, and powers appendant.

A power is *collateral* if the powerholder owns no property interest in the appointive property.

A power is a *power in gross* if the powerholder has a property interest in the appointive property that cannot be affected by the exercise of the power. A power of appointment over the remainder interest, held by the life tenant, is a typical example.

A *power appendant* arises where the powerholder has a property interest in the appointive property that can be affected by the exercise of the power. In other words, the power of appointment purports to authorize the powerholder to divest the powerholder's own property interest and confer it on someone else. A purported exercise of a power appendant is actually a transfer of the powerholder's own property interest.

The following examples illustrate the categories.

Example 10.4: G transferred land "to *A* for life, remainder to such person or persons as *P* shall appoint; in default of appointment, remainder to *B*."

P holds a collateral power. *P* has no
in the appointive property. *P* simply has a
power of appointment.

Example 10.5: *G* transferred land "to *A* for
life, remainder to such person or persons as *A*
shall by will appoint; in default of appointment,
remainder to *B*."

A holds a power in gross. *A* has an interest in
the property (a life estate) but the life estate
cannot be affected by *A*'s testamentary power.

Example 10.6: *G* transferred land "to such
persons as *A* shall appoint, and until and in
default of appointment, to *A* and her heirs."

A has a power appendant. If *A* executes an
instrument purporting to exercise the power,
the instrument is construed as a conveyance of
A's owned interest. Put differently: the transfer
of the land occurs by *A*'s action as its owner,
not as the powerholder of a power.

§ 10.4   Invalid Powers

A power of appointment is invalid if (1) the
permissible appointees are not ascertainable, or (2)
the power violates the Rule Against Perpetuities.

A power of appointment is invalid if it the
permissible appointees are not ascertainable—in

other words, the permissible appointees are so indefinite that it is impossible to identify any person to whom the powerholder can appoint. But if the powerholder can appoint to at least one person who fits the donor's description, courts typically uphold the power.

Example 10.7: G transferred land "to A for life, remainder to such of A's friends as A may designate by his will, and in default of such designation, to X Charity."

The objects of the power—A's "friends"—are sufficiently identifiable by the powerholder (A) that a valid appointment to one or more of them may be made. See Restatement 3d of Property § 18.1 illus. 15.

Powers of appointment are subject to the Rule Against Perpetuities. A power that *violates the Rule* is invalid and cannot be validly exercised. The question of whether a power violates the Rule is discussed in Chapter 14.

§ 10.5 Creating a Power: The Problem of Ambiguous Language

A donor creates a power of appointment "by a transfer that manifests an intent to create a power of appointment." Restatement 3d of Property §

18.1; see also Uniform Powers of Appointment Act § 201(a). The intent can be manifested by the donor either expressly or by implication. No particular language is necessary; the words "power of appointment" or "appoint" need not be used.

> *Example 10.8:* G transferred property "to *A* for life, remainder, if *A* dies intestate, to *B*."
>
> This might be construed as implying a general power in *A* to appoint by will. See Restatement 3d of Property § 18.1 cmt. g; Simes & Smith on Future Interests § 892.

Different courts have construed recurring ambiguous dispositive patterns differently and have reached results that are difficult to reconcile. When, for example, property is devised to a devisee "to be disposed of in [the devisee's] discretion," or words of similar import, a court might adopt one of three interpretations. One is that the devisee takes an absolute-ownership interest on the theory that the added language is without legal effect. A second interpretation views the language as negating ownership and creating only a power of appointment. A third interpretation, appearing in the case law where the devisee is a fiduciary (e.g., the decedent's executor), is that the language creates a mandatory power requiring the fiduciary to distribute the property, with the power held invalid if the class of objects is not sufficiently definite for the fiduciary to perform this task.

Another recurring and perplexing dispositive pattern is the devise to someone for life, remainder to the life tenant's "executors and administrators" or "estate" or some similar phrase. Courts have had great difficulty in deciding the import of this type of devise. Some courts hold that the life tenant takes a general power of appointment. Other courts hold that the life tenant takes a remainder interest. If the remainder to the life tenant's "executors and administrators" is conditioned on some event, such as "income to *A* for life, and if *A* dies with issue, to *A*'s executors and administrators," other possible interpretations arise. One possibility is that the language created a remainder interest in *A*'s issue. Another possibility is that *A* took a nongeneral power. Still another possibility is that *A* received a remainder in fee (in addition to the life estate) on condition that *A* leaves issue.

From the drafting perspective, these ambiguities should be avoided. Powers of appointment should be created using clear and express language.

CHAPTER 11

WHO OWNS THE APPOINTIVE PROPERTY?

§ 11.1   Donors and "Relation Back"

As a technical matter, there is no doubt that the powerholder of a power of appointment is not the owner of the appointive property. The conventional distinction between beneficial ownership and a power of appointment is stated in Restatement 3d of Property § 17.1 cmt. c:

> The beneficial owner of an interest in property ordinarily has the power to transfer ownership interests in or confer powers of appointment over that property to or on others by probate or nonprobate transfer.... By contrast, a power of appointment traditionally confers the authority to designate recipients of

beneficial ownership interests in or confer powers of appointment over property that the powerholder does not own.

Upon the exercise of a power of appointment, the *doctrine of relation back* provides that the appointed property passes directly from the donor to the appointee. The powerholder's appointment is deemed to relate back to and become part of the *donor's* original instrument. The powerholder is viewed as the donor's agent, as it were; an appointment retroactively fills in the blanks in the original instrument.

Example 11.1: G transferred property in trust, providing for "income to *A* for life, remainder to such of *A*'s descendants as *A* shall appoint." *A* makes an inter vivos appointment to his child, *C*.

Under the doctrine of relation back, *A*'s appointment is viewed as changing *G*'s original disposition to read: "income to *A* for life, remainder to *C*."

Technical ownership aside, when it comes to the rights of the powerholder's creditors or surviving spouse, the law does not always follow the relation-back doctrine.[1] The likelihood that the powerholder will be treated as the owner of the appointive property is greater in the case of a reserved power—where the donor of the power is also the powerholder of the power—as distinguished from a power conferred on the powerholder by another. We consider these issues in the remaining sections of this chapter.

§ 11.2   Rights of the Powerholder's Creditors

The rights of the powerholder's creditors depend on whether the power was reserved or whether it was created in the powerholder by another.

If a *reserved* power of appointment was created

---

[1] This statement is also true with respect to federal taxation. The application of federal tax laws to the various kinds of powers of appointment is complicated and beyond the scope of this *Nutshell*. The following is offered as a general summary. If the donor and powerholder are the same person, in other words the donor has reserved in himself a power of appointment, then federal tax laws treat the donor-powerholder as still owning the appointive property, irrespective of whether the power is general or nongeneral. If the donor and powerholder are not the same person, in other words the power was conferred upon the powerholder by another, federal tax laws treat the powerholder as the owner of the appointive property only if the power is general, not if the power is nongeneral.

in a transfer deemed to be in fraud of creditors, the appointive assets can be subjected to the donor-powerholder's debts. See Uniform Powers of Appointment Act § 501(b); Restatement 3d of Property § 22.1 cmt. b. A transfer is in fraud of creditors, according to § 4(a) of the Uniform Fraudulent Transfers Act, if the transfer was made (1) "with actual intent to hinder, delay, or defraud" or (2) "without receiving a reasonably equivalent value in exchange for the transfer" and the transferor "(i) was engaged or was about to engage in a business or a transaction for which the remaining assets of the [transferor] were unreasonably small in relation to the business or transaction; or (ii) intended to incur, or believed or reasonably should have believed that he would incur, debts beyond his ability to pay as they became due."

Even if the transfer was not in fraud of creditors, the appointive assets are typically subject to the claims of the donor-powerholder's creditors if the reserved power is general. See Restatement 3d of Property § 22.2; see also Uniform Powers of Appointment Act § 501(d) (providing that the appointive property is subject to a claim of a creditor of: (1) the powerholder if the reserved power is general and presently exercisable and (2) the powerholder's estate, to the extent the estate is insufficient and subject to the right of a decedent to direct the source from which liabilities are paid, if the power is general and exercisable at death). It makes no difference whether the debt was incurred before or after the transfer creating the power. See Restatement 3d of Property § 22.2 cmt. a.

Example 11.2: G transferred land "to A for life, remainder to such persons as G shall appoint, and in default of appointment, to B." G has incurred substantial debts.

G's creditors can reach the remainder.

Until recent years, an anomaly existed with respect to a reserved power to revoke, such as that contained in a revocable inter vivos trust. The first Restatement of Property excluded powers to revoke from the definition of the term "power of appointment," making inapplicable the rule that a reserved power of appointment subjects the appointive assets to the claims of the donor-powerholder's creditors. See Restatement of Property § 318(2) and cmt. i. In line with this view, courts and authorities held that trust assets of a revocable trust were exempt from the claims of the settlor's creditors. Restatement 2d of Trusts § 330 cmt. o. Recent statutes and cases, however, have adopted the opposite rule: revocable trusts can be reached by the settlor's creditors. See *State Street Bank & Trust Co. v. Reiser*, 7 Mass.App.Ct. 633, 389 N.E.2d 768 (1979). This new understanding has been adopted by the Restatements 2d and 3d of Property, and the Uniform Powers of Appointment Act, which include powers to revoke in the definition of a power of appointment. See, e.g., Uniform Powers of Appointment Act § 102(13) and the accompanying Comment; Restatement 3d of Property § 17.1 cmt. e. Under modern law, therefore, the creditors of the settlor of a revocable trust are entitled to have their claims satisfied out of trust assets. See Restatement 3d of Trusts § 25 cmt. e; Uniform Trust Code § 505(a)(1).

Example 11.3: G transferred property to *T*, as trustee of *G*'s revocable inter vivos trust, to pay "income to *A* for life, and at *A*'s death to deliver the trust assets to *B*." *G* has incurred substantial debts.

Under modern law, *G*'s creditors can reach the property in the trust.

With respect to powers *created in the powerholder by another*, the majority view at common law is that the powerholder's creditors can reach the appointive property if the power is general *and* the powerholder exercises the power, either inter vivos or by will.[2] The Restatement 3d of Property, however, takes a different view, providing that the creditors can reach the property if the power is general and presently exercisable (whether or not exercised) *and* only to the extent the powerholder's own property is insufficient to satisfy the creditors' claims. See Restatement 3d of Property § 22.3. This view is adopted by Uniform Powers of Appointment Act § 502(a), which additionally provides that creditors of the powerholder's *estate* can reach property subject to a general power exercisable at death, to the extent the estate is insufficient and subject to the right of a decedent to direct the source from which liabilities are paid.

---

[2] In most jurisdictions this rule applies only to the extent that the powerholder's exercise was an effective exercise. A few states, however, follow the view that an ineffective exercise entitles the powerholder's creditors to reach the appointive assets. Note that even in the states adhering to the prevailing view, there are circumstances in which an ineffective exercise has the effect under state property law of including the appointive assets in the powerholder's probate estate (see § 13.6), at which point the assets become the powerholder's for all purposes, including creditors' rights.

Example 11.4: G transferred land "to A for life, remainder to such persons as X shall appoint, and in default of appointment, to B." X has incurred substantial debts.

According to the majority view at common law, X's creditors can reach the remainder only if X exercises the power. According to the Uniform Powers of Appointment Act and the Restatement 3d of Property, X's creditors can reach the remainder whether or not X exercises the power, but only to the extent that X's own assets are insufficient to satisfy the creditors' claims.

If the power is nongeneral, the basic rule at common law, in the Restatement 3d of Property, and in the Uniform Powers of Appointment Act is that the powerholder's creditors cannot reach the appointive assets. See Uniform Powers of Appointment Act § 504(a); Restatement 3d of Property § 22.1.

Example 11.5: G transferred land "to A for life, remainder to such charities as X shall appoint, and in default of appointment, to B." X has incurred substantial debts.

X's creditors cannot reach the remainder, because the power is nongeneral.

A few states have enacted legislation that affects the rights of creditors of a powerholder of a power created by another. The laws are not uniform; some expand the rights of the powerholder's creditors, others restrict them. It is important to be aware of any such statute in your state.

A final word may be offered on the federal bankruptcy code, which implies that general powers pass to the powerholder's trustee in bankruptcy; nongeneral powers clearly do not. See 11 U.S.C. § 541(b)(1).

§ 11.3   Rights of the Powerholder's Surviving Spouse

The elective-share rights of the powerholder's surviving spouse depend on whether the power of appointment was reserved or whether it was created in the powerholder by another.

We begin with *reserved* powers. The traditional rule (noted in § 8.3) is that the surviving spouse's elective share applies only to the decedent's probate estate. This typically excludes property subject to a power to revoke or to a reserved power of appointment. A growing number of cases have held that the decedent's attempt during lifetime to transfer property into a revocable trust was a fraudulent or illusory transfer, hence void, rendering the property subject to the elective share.

Example 11.6: G transferred almost all of his assets into a revocable trust of which he was not a beneficiary. The beneficiaries were *G*'s mistress, *M*, for her life, then a remainder in *M*'s then-living descendants. Later *G* died, survived by *M* and by *G*'s spouse, *S*.

Under the traditional law, *S* has no right to an elective share in the trust assets, unless a court would be willing to take the step of declaring *G*'s transfer fraudulent or illusory.

The Restatement 3d of Property provides that the surviving spouse's elective-share rights do extend to property subject to a reserved power (which includes a power to revoke) if the power is either (1) general and presently exercisable by the powerholder immediately before death, or (2) general and testamentary. See Restatement 3d of Property § 23.1. The Restatement's position was adopted in *Sieh v. Sieh*, 713 N.W.2d 194 (Iowa 2006). (The Uniform Probate Code follows a similar approach, except that a testamentary power must have been reserved during the marriage. See

Uniform Probate Code §§ 2-205(1)(A), 2-205(2)(B)).

Example 11.7: Same facts as the previous example, except that the applicable law is (1) the Restatement 3d of Property or (2) the Uniform Probate Code.

Under either the Restatement 3d of Property or the Uniform Probate Code, the trust assets are subject to *S*'s elective-share rights.

Example 11.8: G transferred almost all of his assets into an irrevocable inter vivos trust of which he was not a beneficiary. The beneficiaries were his mistress, *M*, for her life, then a remainder in such persons as *G* may by will appoint, and in default of appointment to *M*'s then-living descendants. Later *G* died, survived by *M* and by *G*'s spouse, *S*.

The Restatement 3d of Property provides that the trust assets will be subject to *S*'s elective-share rights. The Uniform Probate Code provides that the trust assets will be subject to *S*'s elective-share rights if the power was reserved during *G*'s marriage to *S*.

With respect to powers *created in the powerholder by another*, the traditional rule is that the surviving spouse of the powerholder cannot reach the appointive property against the powerholder's wishes. This is true whether the power is general or nongeneral, presently exercisable or testamentary, exercised or unexercised. The explanation offered is that the surviving spouse's elective-share claim is against the powerholder's probate estate, and the appointive assets are not owned beneficially by the powerholder. The current version of the Uniform Probate Code, promulgated in 1990, broke new ground by including in the augmented estate "property over which the decedent alone, immediately before death, held a presently exercisable general power of appointment" regardless of when or by whom the power was created. Uniform Probate Code § 2-205(1)(A). This is essentially the same rule now promulgated in Restatement 3d of Property § 23.1(1).[3]

Example 11.9: G transferred land "to *A* for life, remainder to such persons as *X* shall appoint, and in default of appointment, to *B*." *X* then died, survived by his spouse, *S*.

---

[3]Restatement 3d of Property § 23.1(1) does not contain the Uniform Probate Code's requirement that the decedent hold the power "alone."

Under traditional law, the land is not subject to S's elective share. The Restatement 3d of Property and the Uniform Probate Code reach the opposite result, on the ground that X's presently exercisable general power gave X ownership of the land in substance if not in form.

CHAPTER 12

EXERCISING A POWER

§ 12.1 Capacity of the Powerholder

An effective appointment can only be made by a powerholder who has the requisite capacity. The capacity to make an effective appointment is the same capacity needed to make an effective transfer of the property if it were owned by the powerholder. See Restatement 3d of Property § 19.8(a); see also Uniform Powers of Appointment Act § 301(1) (requiring the instrument exercising the power to be valid under applicable law).

The capacity to make inter vivos and testamentary transfers is described in the Restatement 3d of Property § 8.1:

> If the donative transfer is in the form of a will, a revocable will substitute, or a revocable gift, the testator or donor must

be capable of knowing and understanding in a general way the nature and extent of his or her property, the natural objects of his or her bounty, and the disposition that he or she is making of that property, and must also be capable of relating these elements to one another and forming an orderly desire regarding the disposition of the property.

If the donative transfer is in the form of an irrevocable gift, the donor must have the mental capacity necessary to make or revoke a will and must also be capable of understanding the effect that the gift may have on the future financial security of the donor and of anyone who may be dependent on the donor.

Consider how these standards would apply to the following example.

Example 12.1: G transferred land "to *A* for life, then to such persons as *A* shall by will appoint, and in default of appointment, to *B*." Believing that there were people living in the trees on the land, *A* signed a will exercising the power of appointment in their favor so that they could be fed. No such tree-people existed.

A lacks the legal capacity to exercise the power of appointment by will. The attempted exercise is invalid, so the land passes at *A*'s death to *B* in fee simple absolute.

§ 12.2   Compliance With Formalities

An appointment must satisfy the formal requirements that would be applicable to a transfer of the property if it were owned by the powerholder. See Uniform Powers of Appointment Act § 301(1); Restatement 3d of Property § 19.9(i). A testamentary appointment, for example, must be contained in a validly executed will.

> *Example 12.2: G* transferred land "to *A* for life, then to such persons as *X* shall appoint, and in default of appointment, to *B*." Later *X* orally proclaimed that the property should pass at *A*'s death to *A*'s daughter, *D*. The applicable statutes require a transfer of land by conveyance or devise in writing.
>
> The attempted exercise of the power of appointment is ineffective.

§ 12.3   Intent to Exercise

A powerholder must manifest an intent to exercise a power in order for the power to be exercised. See Uniform Powers of Appointment

Act § 301(2)(A); Restatement 3d of Property § 19.1(1). The recommended method for exercising a power of appointment is by a specific-exercise clause:

> I exercise the power of appointment conferred upon me by [my mother's will of [date]] as follows: I appoint [fill in details of appointment].

Unfortunately, the recommended method is not always used. Often, a so-called blanket-exercise clause is used. A blanket-exercise clause purports to exercise "any power of appointment" the powerholder may have. Blanket-exercise clauses are typically found in blending clauses, which blend the appointive property with the powerholder's own property:

> All the residue of my estate, including any property over which I have a power of appointment, I give as follows: [fill in details of devise].

(Note that a blending clause need not entail a blanket exercise. A clause providing "All the residue of my estate, including the property over which I have a power of appointment under [my mother's will], I give as follows" is a blending clause with a specific exercise, not a blending clause with a blanket exercise.)

Blanket-exercise clauses express the powerholder's intent to exercise a power of appointment. They are not recommended, however, because they can raise a question about whether the exercise of the power complies with the formality of a specific reference requirement commonly imposed by donors (see § 12.4) and because they may subject the appointive property to the claims of the powerholder's creditors (see § 11.2 note 2 and § 13.6).

In the absence of an express exercise of a power, an intent by the powerholder to exercise the power can be implied. In the leading case of *Blagge v. Miles*, 1 Story 426, 3 F. Cas. 559 (C.C. Mass. 1841), the court described circumstances giving rise to an implied exercise:

> Three classes of cases have been held to be sufficient demonstrations of an intended execution of a power: (1) Where there has been some reference in the will, or other instrument, to the power; (2) or a reference to the property, which is the subject, on which it is to be executed; (3) or, where the provision in the will or

other instrument, executed by the powerholder of the power, would otherwise be ineffectual, or a mere nullity; in other words, it would have no operation, except as an execution of the power.

The majority view at common law is that a residuary clause or other clause referring generally to "my estate" or "my property" does not exercise a power of appointment unless other facts establish intent.

A minority of jurisdictions, however, follows the so-called Massachusetts view, which rebuttably presumes that a residuary clause was intended to exercise a general power even though the clause makes no reference to powers. Massachusetts itself abrogated that view by adopting a statute similar to the pre-1990 version of Uniform Probate Code § 2-610, which codified the majority common-law view. See Mass. Gen. Laws ch. 191 § 1(A)(4).

The Uniform Powers of Appointment Act, the Uniform Probate Code, and the Restatement 3d of Property adopt a variation of the minority view. Under Uniform Powers of Appointment Act § 302(b), Uniform Probate Code § 2-608, and Restatement 3d of Property § 19.4, a general power is presumed exercised by a residuary clause, but only if the donor failed to create a gift in default of appointment (or, under the Uniform Powers of Appointment Act and the Restatement 3d of Property, if the donor provided a gift-in-default clause but the clause was ineffective). The aim is to avoid the appointive property returning to the donor's estate, which would need to be reopened if, as is likely, the donor predeceased the powerholder.

Example 12.3: G devised land "to A for life, then to such persons as A shall by will appoint." A later died with a will providing for the disposition of "all my property to C."

Under the majority view at common law, A has not exercised the power of appointment. At A's death, the property reverts to G (i.e., G's successors in interest).

Under the minority view at common law, the Restatement 3d of Property, the Uniform Powers of Appointment Act, and the Uniform Probate Code, A has exercised the power of appointment. It is not necessary to reopen G's estate to identify G's successors in interest. Instead, the land passes at A's death to C.

§ 12.4   Specific-Reference Requirements

In creating powers of appointment, it has become common practice for donors to provide that the power can only be exercised by language that specifically refers to the power. Specific-reference requirements came into use to prevent the adverse tax consequences that would arise from the inadvertent exercise of pre-1942 powers. They are still in common use today even though the tax treatment of post-1942 powers is different.[1]

A frequently litigated question is whether a particular powerholder has made a sufficiently specific reference. The question typically arises when the powerholder has used a blanket-exercise clause—a clause referring simply to "any property over which I have a power of appointment."

There is a split of authority on this question. Some judicial decisions state that a blanket-

---

[1] For general powers created in the powerholder by another on or before October 21, 1942, the value of the appointive property is taxed in the powerholder's estate only if the power is exercised. For such powers created after that date, the value of the appointive property is taxed in the powerholder's estate regardless of whether the power is exercised. See IRC § 2041.

exercise clause does not satisfy a specific-reference requirement. See *First Nat'l Bank v. Walker*, 607 S.W.2d 469 (Tenn. 1980). Other decisions as well as § 304 of the Uniform Powers of Appointment Act, § 2-704 of the Uniform Probate Code, and § 19.10 cmt. d of the Restatement 3d of Property take a different view, that a blanket-exercise clause can satisfy a specific-reference requirement, especially where there is evidence that the powerholder knew of and intended to exercise the power and where there is no evidence that the donor intended to be so restrictive as to prevent any exercise not referring specifically to the power or the creating instrument. See *Motes/Henes Trust v. Motes*, 297 Ark. 380, 761 S.W.2d 938 (1988). Consider the following example.

Example 12.4: G devised property in trust "to *T*, to pay the income to *A* for life, then to deliver the trust property to such persons as *A* shall by will appoint, specifically referring to this power of appointment, and in default of exercise, to *B*." Later *A* executed a will, intending to exercise the power. The will's residuary clause gives "all of my property, including any property over which I may have a power of appointment, to *X*."

Under the approach of some states, *A* has not effectively exercised the power of appointment; the property instead passes at *A*'s death to *B* in fee simple absolute. Under the approach of other states, Uniform Powers of Appointment Act § 304, Uniform Probate Code § 2-704, and Restatement 3d of Property § 19.10 cmt. d, the opposite result is reached: the exercise is effective because there is evidence that *A* intended to exercise the power and no evidence that *G* intended to prevent an exercise in this fashion.

We prefer the flexible presumptions of uniform law and the Restatement 3d of Property over any bright-line rule. As stated in Uniform Powers of Appointment Act :

> *§ 304. Substantial Compliance with Donor-Imposed Formal Requirement*
>
> A powerholder's substantial compliance with a formal requirement of appointment imposed by the donor, including a requirement that the instrument exercising the power of appointment make reference or specific reference to the power, is sufficient if: (1) the powerholder knows of and intends to

exercise the power; and (2) the powerholder's manner of attempted exercise of the power does not impair a material purpose of the donor in imposing the requirement.

CHAPTER 13

EFFECTIVENESS OF THE APPOINTMENT

§ 13.1   Deceased Appointees

An exercise of a power of appointment in favor of a deceased person is ineffective, except as saved by an antilapse statute. See Uniform Powers of Appointment Act § 306; Restatement 3d of Property § 19.12. (For students who have not yet covered this material in a course in Trusts and Estates: antilapse statutes typically provide that if a devisee fails to survive the testator, a substitute gift is created in the devisee's descendants who survive the testator. The statutes usually apply only to devisees who are relatives or specified relatives of the testator.)

The Uniform Probate Code's antilapse statute expressly applies to the exercise of a power of appointment, by defining "devisee" as including "an appointee under a power of appointment exercised by the testator's will" if the appointee is a "grandparent, a descendant of a grandparent or a stepchild of either the testator or the donor of the power." Uniform Probate Code § 2-603(a)(4), (b).

Antilapse statutes in states that have not adopted the Uniform Probate Code are commonly silent as to whether they apply to the exercise of a power of appointment. The Restatement 3d of Property recommends that such statutes "should nevertheless be construed to apply to such an exercise, unless the applicable statute expressly excludes appointments." Restatement 3d of Property § 19.12 cmt. b.

Consider the following example.

Example 13.1: (1) G devised land "to *A* for life, remainder to such persons as *A* shall by will appoint, and in default of appointment, to *B*."

(2) G devised land "to A for life, remainder to such of A's descendants as A shall by will appoint, and in default of appointment, to B."

A executed a will exercising her power of appointment in favor of her son, S. S predeceased A, leaving three of S's children who survived A.

In both Variations, an antilapse statute would (or should be read to) create a substitute appointment in S's children who survived A.

The Uniform Probate Code and the Restatement 3d of Property provide that the substitute gift is not defeated merely because the substitute takers are not permissible appointees of the power. Uniform Probate Code § 2-603(b)(5) states that "a surviving descendant of a deceased appointee of a power of appointment can be substituted for the appointee ... whether or not the descendant is an object of the power." Accord Restatement 3d of Property §§ 5.5 cmt. *l*, 19.12 cmt. e.

Example 13.2: Same facts as Variation (2) above, except that the permissible appointees of the power are not A's "descendants" but A's "children."

Under the Uniform Probate Code and Restatement 3d of Property, the substitute appointment in S's children (A's grandchildren) is still created, even though the nongeneral power was limited to A's children.

§ 13.2   The Creation of Interests Short of Absolute Ownership

A question that sometimes arises is whether the powerholder of a power of appointment must appoint the property absolutely (if land, in fee simple absolute) or whether the powerholder can create limited or future interests in the appointees. The answer is that, absent the donor's manifested contrary intention, the powerholder may create limited or future interests in the appointees. See Uniform Powers of Appointment Act § 305; Restatement 3d of Property §§ 19.13, 19.14. Furthermore, if the power is a general power, the powerholder may create limited or future interests even where the donor has explicitly prohibited it, because attempting to enforce the prohibition would be useless; the powerholder could simply appoint to himself outright and then transfer an interest short of fee simple absolute. See Uniform Powers of Appointment Act § 305(a) and the accompanying Comment; Restatement 3d of Property §§ 19.13(a), 19.15 cmt. b.

Example 13.3: G transferred land "to A for life, remainder to such persons as A shall appoint, and in default of appointment, to B." A exercised the power to create a life estate in his son, S, followed by a remainder in S's descendants who survive S.

A has validly exercised the power. Because the power is general, this exercise would be valid even if G had expressly restricted the exercise to transfers in fee simple absolute.

§ 13.3   The Creation of a New Power

The powerholder of a general power can confer a power of appointment, general or nongeneral, on the appointee. See Uniform Powers of Appointment Act § 305; Restatement 3d of Property § 19.13 cmt. f.

With respect to a nongeneral power, the better view is that the powerholder can create a general power in the appointee. See Uniform Powers of Appointment Act § 305(c)(2); Restatement 3d of Property § 19.14 cmt. g. After all, the powerholder could have appointed outright to the appointee, and conferring a general power is the equivalent.

The powerholder of a nongeneral power can create a nongeneral power in anyone, as long as the permissible appointees of the second power do not include anyone who is not a permissible appointee of the first. This limitation may seem odd, but it is explained by the theory that the original powerholder is, in effect, delegating to the second powerholder the final selection of appointees. Uniform Powers of Appointment Act § 305(c); Restatement 3d of Property § 19.14 cmt. g.

Example 13.4: G transferred land "to *A* for life, remainder to such of *A*'s descendants as *A* shall by will appoint, and in default of appointment, to *B*."

(1) *A*'s will exercised the power of appointment by devising the land "to such persons as my son, *S*, shall appoint."

(2) *A*'s will exercised the power of appointment by devising the land "to such of my descendants as my neighbor, *N*, shall appoint."

(3) *A*'s will exercised the power of appointment by devising the land "to such charities as my son, *S*, shall appoint."

According to the Uniform Powers of Appointment Act and the Restatement 3d of Property, *A*'s exercise is valid in Variations (1) and (2) but not in Variation (3). The latter result occurs because the permissible appointees of *S*'s nongeneral power are not permissible appointees of *A*'s nongeneral power.

§ 13.4   Appointments to Impermissible Appointees

The exercise of a nongeneral power[1] in favor of a person who is not a permissible appointee is ineffective. See Uniform Powers of Appointment Act § 307(a). This is true whether the appointment is made directly to the impermissible appointee or whether it is made indirectly—in other words, to a permissible appointee for the benefit of an impermissible appointee. Such an indirect appointment is called a *fraud on the power*. See Uniform Powers of Appointment Act § 307(b); Restatement 3d of Property § 19.16.

Example 13.5: *G* transferred land "to *A* for life, remainder to such of *A*'s descendants as *A* shall appoint, otherwise to *B*." *A* exercised the power in favor of her husband, *H*.

A's exercise is ineffective. At *A*'s death, the land passes to *B* in fee simple absolute.

---

[1] Or some narrow general powers—e.g., a power exercisable only in favor of the powerholder's creditors.

§ 13.5   Appointments to Takers in Default

There is disagreement among the cases as to the effectiveness of an appointment to someone who would receive the same property anyway as a taker in default. Some cases hold that such an appointment is ineffective, because an exercise in conformity with the taker-in-default's interest is a nullity. The Uniform Powers of Appointment Act and the Restatement 3d of Property agree. In the words of § 313 of the Uniform Act: "If a powerholder makes an appointment to a taker in default of appointment and the appointee would have taken the property under a gift-in-default clause had the property not been appointed, the power of appointment is deemed not to have been exercised, and the appointee takes under the clause." Accord, Restatement 3d of Property § 19.25.

The capacity in which the person takes, as appointee or as taker in default, is of no great concern to the person taking. The significance of whether the appointment is effective lies elsewhere. The question usually arises in cases of general powers and the claims of the powerholder's creditors, usually creditors of the powerholder's estate. By the majority common-law view, an ineffective appointment of a general power does not allow creditors to reach the appointive assets. (See § 11.2 note 2.)

Example 13.6: G transferred land "to *A* for life, remainder to such persons, including *X*'s estate, as *X* shall by will appoint, and in default of appointment, to *B*." *X* died having accumulated substantial debts. He purported to exercise the power of appointment in his will, in favor of *B*.

Whether the exercise is deemed effective depends upon the jurisdiction. If the exercise is deemed ineffective, the majority of jurisdictions would then hold that the creditors of *X*'s estate may not reach the land.

§ 13.6 Failure to Exercise; Ineffective Exercise

If a powerholder fails to exercise the power, the appointive assets pass to the takers in default. Uniform Powers of Appointment Act §§ 310(1), 311(1); Restatement 3d of Property § 17.2(f). If there is no gift-in-default clause, or to the extent the gift-in-default clause is ineffective, what happens to the property depends on whether the power is general or nongeneral.

If a *general* power is *unexercised*, the Uniform Powers of Appointment Act provides that, if the powerholder merely failed to exercise the power, the appointive property passes (1) to the powerholder if living and a permissible appointee, or (2) if the powerholder is an impermissible appointee or deceased, to the powerholder's estate if the estate is a permissible appointee. However, if the powerholder released the power (or if there is no taker under the earlier provisions), the appointive property reverts to the donor (or the donor's transferee or successor in interest). Uniform Powers of Appointment Act § 310(2). Accord, Restatement 3d of Property § 19.22. This approach contrasts with the earlier rule of the Restatement 2d of Property, which had simply provided that the appointive property reverts to the donor (or the donor's successors in interest). See Restatement 2d of Property § 24.1.

If a *nongeneral* power is *unexercised* or if the appointment is *ineffective*, the Uniform Powers of Appointment Act and the Restatements 3d and 2d of Property provide that the appointive property passes to the permissible appointees of the power if they are a defined and limited class or, if not, it reverts to the donor (or the donor's transferee or successor in interest). See Uniform Powers of

Appointment Act §311(2); Restatement 3d of Property § 19.23; Restatement 2d of Property § 24.2. Two different theories are employed to reach this result. Some courts hold that the powerholder of a nongeneral power with a defined and limited class of permissible appointees has the duty to exercise the power, i.e., that the power is a power in trust (also called an imperative or mandatory power), and the court will not permit the permissible appointees to suffer by the negligence of the powerholder. Other courts imply a gift in default in favor of the permissible appointees. The Restatement 3d of Property and the Uniform Powers of Appointment Act adopt the implied-gift-in-default theory. See Restatement 3d of Property § 19.23(b); Uniform Powers of Appointment Act § 311(2) and the accompanying Comment.

Example 13.7: The permissible appointees of *A*'s nongeneral power are *A*'s children; there is no express gift in default. *A* either dies without exercising the power or makes an ineffective appointment.

Because the permissible appointees—*A*'s children—are a defined and limited class, the appointive property passes to *A*'s children who survive *A* (and substituted takers for a deceased child, if an antilapse statute applies). If, however, there are no permissible appointees to whom the property can pass (for example, if *A* is not survived by any children, or by any descendants if an antilapse statute applies), the appointive property reverts to the donor (or the donor's successors in interest).

Example 13.8: The permissible appointees of *A*'s nongeneral power are anyone in the world except *A*, *A*'s estate, and the creditors of either. *A* either dies without exercising the power or makes an ineffective appointment.

Because the permissible appointees are not a defined and limited class, the appointive property reverts to the donor (or the donor's successors in interest).

There is a special rule governing the *ineffective* exercise (as opposed to failure to exercise) of a *general* power. The traditional result is that the property passes to the takers in default or, if none, to the donor (or the donor's successors in interest). If, however, the powerholder's appointment manifests an intent to assume control of the property for all purposes and not merely for the limited purpose of giving effect to the expressed appointment, some courts have applied the so-called *capture doctrine*, which means that the appointive property passes to the powerholder or the powerholder's estate.

The powerholder's intent to assume control of the property "for all purposes" is manifested (and the capture doctrine is triggered) by: (1) a blanket-exercise clause, described in § 12.3; (2) a residuary clause that presumptively demonstrates an intent to exercise the power, pursuant to a statute or rule of common law; (3) a residuary clause that demonstrates an intent to exercise the power because the powerholder's estate is insufficient to satisfy the powerholder's devises; or (4) in the view of some but not all courts, an appointment in trust.[2]

The Uniform Powers of Appointment Act and the Restatement 3d of Property adopt a "modern variation" of the capture doctrine. The ineffective exercise of a general power results in the property passing under the gift-in-default clause or, to the extent the gift-in-default clause is nonexistent or ineffective, to the powerholder (or the

---

[2]To protect against the capture doctrine, donors should introduce the gift-in-default clause with the phrase: "To the extent the powerholder does not expressly exercise this power of appointment effectively,..."

powerholder's estate) if a permissible appointee; if not, the property reverts to the donor (or the donor's successors in interest.) See Uniform Powers of Appointment Act § 309. Neither the Uniform Powers of Appointment Act nor the Restatement 3d conducts an inquiry into whether the powerholder manifested an intention to assume control of the property for all purposes. See, e.g., Restatement 3d of Property § 19.21.

§ 13.7   Releases of Powers

The Uniform Powers of Appointment Act and the Restatement 3d of Property declare that all powers of appointment, general and nongeneral, testamentary and presently exercisable, are releasable in whole or in part, unless the donor has effectively manifested an intent that the power not be releasable. See Uniform Powers of Appointment Act § 402; Restatement 3d of Property §§ 20.1 and 20.2

If the donor of a power expressly provides that the power cannot be released, the donor's intention may not be effective. The restriction must still be examined under the rules governing restraints on alienation. See Uniform Powers of Appointment Act § 402 and the accompanying Comment; Restatement 3d of Property §§ 20.1 cmts. c & d,

20.2 cmts. b & c.

The release of a general power of appointment causes the appointive property to pass under the gift-in-default clause or, if none or to the extent the clause is ineffective, to revert to the donor (or the donor's successors in interest). See Uniform Powers of Appointment Act § 310; Restatement 3d of Property § 19.22.

The release of a nongeneral power of appointment causes the appointive property to pass under the gift-in-default clause or, if none or to the extent the clause is ineffective, to the permissible appointees if they are a defined and limited class or, if not, to revert to the donor (or the donor's successors in interest). See Uniform Powers of Appointment Act § 311; Restatement 3d of Property § 19.23.

CHAPTER 14

POWERS AND THE RULE AGAINST PERPETUITIES

§ 14.1   The Rule and "Relation Back"

Recall the *doctrine of relation back* from Chapter 11: the powerholder's appointment is deemed to relate back to and become part of the donor's original instrument. As we saw in that chapter, the doctrine is sometimes followed, sometimes not.

When relation back is not followed, it is usually because the nature of the power puts the powerholder's relationship to the appointive property close enough in substance to that of an outright owner that, for the purposes of the particular question involved, the property should be treated as if owned by the powerholder.

The Rule Against Perpetuities follows or rejects relation back on this basis. For perpetuity purposes, as we shall see, the relation back theory is generally followed for nongeneral powers and for general testamentary powers but rejected for presently exercisable general powers.

With the above background in mind, we can now consider how the Rule Against Perpetuities applies to powers of appointment. It is important to distinguish between the validity of the *power itself* and the validity of the *exercise* of the power. If a power of appointment itself violates the Rule Against Perpetuities, the power is invalid. If the power itself is valid, it may be exercised in such a way that creates property interests that may violate the Rule and be invalid.

§ 14.2   Presently Exercisable General Powers

Under the common-law Rule and the Uniform Rule, a general power that is presently exercisable is treated as the equivalent of a *vested* property interest *in the powerholder* (rejecting relation back). As a vested interest, the power itself is not subject to either Rule.

Example 14.1: G devised land "to my son *A* for life, remainder to such persons as *A* shall appoint, and in default of appointment, to *B*."

A's presently exercisable general power of appointment is treated as vested, hence not subject to the common-law Rule or to the Uniform Rule.

Under the Rule Against Perpetuities as reformulated in the Restatement 3d of Property, the powerholder of a power of appointment—whether general or nongeneral, presently exercisable or testamentary—is a "beneficiary" of a "donative disposition of property." See Restatement 3d of Property § 27.1 cmt. d(2). Accordingly, the power is subject to judicial modification under § 27.2 if it does not terminate on or before the expiration of the generations-based perpetuity period in § 27.1(b).

Example 14.2: Same facts as in Example 14.1.

A's presently exercisable general power of appointment is valid because it will terminate at *A*'s death. This is within the generations-based perpetuity period of the Restatement 3d of Property.

Even if the power is valid at common law, under the Uniform Rule, or under the Rule as reformulated in the Restatement 3d of Property (whichever Rule governs in the relevant jurisdiction), one must still determine the validity of the power's *exercise*.

In determining this, for purposes of the Rule at common law, the *powerholder* (not the donor) is considered to have created the appointed interests. Put differently: the exercise is treated as if the powerholder first exercised the power in his or her own favor and then created the appointed interests out of owned property. Consequently, the appointed interests are created, for purposes of the Rule, when the exercise of the power becomes effective. (On "time of creation" see § 5.7 above.)

The only change in the above analysis effected by the Uniform Rule is that an exercise that would have been invalid at common law is not initially invalid, but instead is subject to wait-and-see. The 90-year period applies in determining the validity of appointed interests that would have been invalid at common law.

Consider the following example.

Example 14.3: A was the income beneficiary of a trust and the powerholder of a presently exercisable general power over the succeeding remainder interest. *A* exercised the power by deed, directing the trustee after *A*'s death to pay the income to *A*'s children in equal shares for the life of the survivor, and upon the death of the last surviving child to pay the corpus of the trust to her then-living grandchildren.

Under the common-law Rule, the validity of the appointed interests depends on whether *A*'s appointment was irrevocable. If *A* reserved a power to revoke the appointment, the appointed interests are deemed created at *A*'s death and are valid. If *A*'s appointment was irrevocable, however, the interests were created when the deed was delivered or otherwise became effective, and the remainder interest in *A*'s grandchildren is invalid.

Under the Uniform Rule, the outcome is the same, except that if *A*'s appointment was irrevocable, the remainder in *A*'s grandchildren is not initially invalid. Instead, it is valid if *A*'s last surviving child dies within 90 years after *A*'s death.

Following the approach at common law, the Restatement 3d of Property treats the powerholder who exercises a presently exercisable general power as the "transferor" (rejecting relation back). See Restatement 3d of Property § 27.1 cmt. j(1). Under the Restatement 3d, then, the trust or other donative disposition created by the exercise of the presently exercisable general power is subject to judicial modification under § 27.2 if the disposition does not terminate on or before the expiration of the generations-based perpetuity period in § 27.1(b).

Example 14.4: Same facts as Example 14.3.

The exercise of A's presently exercisable general power is valid because the interests in trust created by A's exercise will terminate at the death of A's last surviving child. This is within the generations-based perpetuity period of the Restatement 3d of Property.

§ 14.3   General   Powers   Not Presently Exercisable Because of a Condition Precedent

If a general power would be presently exercisable but for the fact that its exercise is subject to a condition precedent, the power is treated by both the common-law Rule and the Uniform Rule as the equivalent of a *nonvested* property interest *in the powerholder* (rejecting relation back). Remember that a power of appointment expires on the powerholder's death (§ 10.2 above), and so a deferral of a power's exercisability until a future time—even a time certain—imposes a condition precedent, the condition precedent being that the powerholder must be alive at that future time.

Under the common-law Rule, a general power not presently exercisable because of a condition precedent is invalid unless the condition precedent must be resolved one way or the other within a life in being plus 21 years. Consequently, an unborn person can be the recipient of a valid general power that becomes presently exercisable upon the powerholder's birth. To be valid, of course, the powerholder's birth must be certain to occur, if it ever occurs, within a life in being plus 21 years.

Under the Uniform Rule, a general power not presently exercisable because of a condition precedent is initially valid if it satisfies the common-law Rule. If it does not satisfy the common-law Rule, however, the power is not automatically invalid. Instead, the power is valid if the condition precedent actually occurs within the 90-year period; if it does not, the disposition can be reformed to make it valid.

These principles are illustrated in the following example.

Example 14.5: G devised land "to my son *A* for life, then to *A*'s first born child for life, then to such persons as *A*'s first born child shall appoint." *G* was survived by *A*, who is childless.

Under the common-law Rule, the general power conferred upon *A*'s first born child is valid. The condition precedent—that *A* have a child—is certain to be resolved one way or the other within *A*'s lifetime; *A* is the validating life. If, however, the relevant language had been "then to such persons as *A*'s first born child shall appoint after reaching age 25," the age contingency would invalidate the general power at common law.

Under the Uniform Rule, the outcome is the same, except that if the power in *A*'s first born child was contingent on reaching age 25, the power would not be initially invalid. Instead, it would be valid if *A*'s first born child reaches age 25 within 90 years after *A*'s death.

Under the Rule Against Perpetuities as reformulated in the Restatement 3d of Property, the powerholder of the power is a "beneficiary" of a "donative disposition of property." See Restatement 3d of Property § 27.1 cmt. d(2). Accordingly, the power is subject to judicial modification under § 27.2 if it does not terminate on or before the expiration of the generations-based perpetuity period in § 27.1(b).

Example 14.6: Same facts as in Example 14.5.

The presently exercisable general power of appointment held by *A*'s first born child is valid because it will terminate at the child's death. This is within the generations-based perpetuity period of the Restatement 3d of Property.

If a general power that was once not presently exercisable because of a condition precedent is valid and becomes presently exercisable, the validity of an exercise is governed by the same principles discussed in § 14.2 above.

§ 14.4   Nongeneral Powers and General Testamentary Powers

To be valid under the common-law Rule, a nongeneral power (whether testamentary or presently exercisable) or a general testamentary power cannot be *exercisable* beyond a life in being plus 21 years.[1] Underpinning this rule is the theory of relation back—the theory that any property interest created by the powerholder's exercise of a nongeneral power or of a general testamentary power is created by the donor *when the donor created the power*. Because no such property interest can vest until the power is exercised, the common-law Rule requires certainty that the power cannot be exercised beyond a life in being plus 21 years.

The Uniform Rule also follows the basic theory of relation back for nongeneral and general testamentary powers. Under the Uniform Rule, a nongeneral power or a general testamentary power that would be valid at common law is valid. The change effected by the Uniform Rule is that a nongeneral or a general testamentary power that would be invalid at common law is not initially

---

[1] Discretionary powers held by fiduciaries (e.g., trustees) are nongeneral powers of appointment for perpetuity purposes. Discretionary fiduciary powers include a trustee's power to invade the corpus of a trust for the benefit of the income beneficiary, or a trustee's power to accumulate the income or pay it out among a group of beneficiaries.

Purely administrative fiduciary powers, such as the power to sell and reinvest trust assets, are not subject to either Rule.

invalid. Instead, the power is valid if it is actually exercised within 90 years after it was created.

Consider the following example.

Example 14.7: (1) G devised land "to my daughter *A* for life, then to *A*'s first born child for life, then to such persons as *A*'s first born child shall by will appoint;" or

(2) G devised land "to my daughter *A* for life, then to *A*'s first born child for life, then to such of *A*'s grandchildren as *A*'s first born child shall appoint."

G was survived by *A*, who is childless.

Under the common-law Rule, the power of appointment conferred upon *A*'s first born child—a general testamentary power in Variation (1), a nongeneral power presently exercisable in Variation (2)—is invalid. The latest possible time of exercise is at the death of *A*'s first born child, who cannot be the validating life because he or she was not "in being" at the creation of the power. The lesson under the common-law Rule is that a nongeneral or general testamentary power cannot validly be conferred on an unborn person, unless a perpetuity saving clause limits the power's exercisability to a life in being plus

21 years.

Under the Uniform Rule, the power in *A*'s first born child is not initially invalid. It is valid if *A*'s first born child exercises the power within 90 years after *G*'s death. Note that a testamentary exercise takes place when the powerholder dies, not when the powerholder signs his or her will. Thus, in Variation (1), *A*'s first born child must die within 90 years after *G*'s death in order for the child's power to be valid. In Variation (2), the child must also die within 90 years after *G*'s death if the child chooses to exercise the power by will rather than by deed.

Under the Rule Against Perpetuities as reformulated in the Restatement 3d of Property, the powerholder of a power is a "beneficiary" of a "donative disposition of property." See Restatement 3d of Property § 27.1 cmt. d(2). Accordingly, the power is subject to judicial modification under § 27.2 if it does not terminate on or before the expiration of the generations-based perpetuity period in § 27.1(b).

Example 14.8: Same facts as in Example 14.7.

The power of appointment in *A*'s first born

child—a general testamentary power in Variation (1), a nongeneral presently exercisable power in Variation (2)—is valid because it will terminate at the death of the child. This is within the generations-based perpetuity period of the Restatement 3d of Property.

If a general testamentary or nongeneral power is valid under the common-law Rule, the Uniform Rule, or the Rule as reformulated in the Restatement 3d of Property (whichever Rule governs in the relevant jurisdiction), it can be validly exercised. Whether or not the exercise *is* valid is the next question.

Both the common-law Rule and the Uniform Rule apply the theory of relation back in determining the validity of interests created by the exercise of these types of powers. Thus, any property interest created by the powerholder's exercise is treated as created by the donor *when the donor created the power.*

Once the time of creation is pinpointed, both the common-law Rule and the Uniform Rule basically apply the same rules to appointed interests as they apply to interests created by an owner of property. At common law, contingent interests must be certain to vest, if at all, within a life in being (at the creation of the power) plus 21 years. Under the Uniform Rule, contingent interests that do not satisfy the common-law Rule are valid if they vest within 90 years after the creation of the power.

Consider the following examples.

Example 14.9: (1) A was the life income beneficiary of a trust and the powerholder of a nongeneral power over the succeeding remainder interest.

(2) A was the life income beneficiary of a trust and the powerholder of a general testamentary power over the succeeding remainder interest

In both cases, the trust was created by the will of *A*'s mother, *G*, who predeceased him. *A* exercised his power by will, directing the income to be paid after his death to his brother *B*'s children for the life of the survivor of them, and upon the death of *B*'s last surviving child, to pay the corpus of the trust to *B*'s then-living grandchildren. *B* predeceased *G*; *B* was survived by his two children, *X* and *Y*, who also survived *G* and *A*.

Under both the common-law Rule and the Uniform Rule, *A*'s appointment in either

Variation is valid. The remainder interest in B's grandchildren was created at G's death when the power was created, not on A's death when the power was exercised. Since B was dead at G's death, the validating lives are X and Y.

Example 14.10: Suppose that in the preceding example A exercised his power by will, directing the income to be paid after his death to his own children for the life of the survivor, and upon the death of A's last surviving child, to pay the corpus of the trust to A's then-living grandchildren. Suppose also that, at G's death, A had two children, X and Y, and that a third child Z was born later. X, Y, and Z all survived A.

Under the common-law Rule, the remainder interest in A's grandchildren is treated as created by G when G died and is therefore invalid.

In Variation (1), where A's power was a nongeneral power, at least one jurisdiction has non-uniform legislation providing that, for perpetuity purposes, the appointed interests were created when A exercised his power, not when his mother created his power. See Del. Code tit. 25 § 501. Under this view, the remainder interest in A's grandchildren would be valid. *A*'s children would be the validating lives.

In Variation (2), where *A*'s power was a general testamentary power, a small number of jurisdictions have non-uniform legislation providing (and at least one common-law court has held) that, for perpetuity purposes, the appointed interests were created when *A* exercised his power, not when his mother created his power. See Del. Code tit. 25 § 501; S.D. Cod. Laws § 43-5-5; Wis. Stat. § 700.16; *Industrial Nat'l Bank v. Barrett*, 101 R.I. 89, 220 A.2d 517 (1966). Again under this view, the remainder interest in *A*'s grandchildren would be valid. *A*'s children would be the validating lives.

Under the Uniform Rule, the remainder interest in *A*'s grandchildren is treated as created when *G* died, not when *A* exercised his power. Unlike the rule at common law, however, the remainder interest is not initially invalid. It is valid if *A*'s last surviving child dies within 90 years after *G*'s death.

The Rule as reformulated in the Restatement 3d of Property similarly applies the theory of relation back to the exercise of a general testamentary or nongeneral power. Under that doctrine, the *donor* of the power is the "transferor" of the trust or other donative disposition created by the exercise of the power. See Restatement 3d of Property § 27.1 cmt. j(2).

Example 14.11: Same facts as in Example 14.9.

In each Variation, the exercise of *A*'s power of appointment is valid under the Rule as reformulated in the Restatement 3d of Property. *G* is considered to be the transferor. The interests in trust created by the exercise of *A*'s power will terminate at the death of the last surviving child of *A*'s brother *B*. This is within the generations-based perpetuity period of the Restatement 3d of Property.

Example 14.12: Same facts as in Example 14.10.

In each Variation, the exercise of *A*'s power of appointment is valid under the Rule as reformulated in the Restatement 3d of Property. *G* is considered to be the transferor. The interests in trust created by the exercise of *A*'s power will terminate at the death of the last surviving child of *A*. This is within the generations-based perpetuity period of the Restatement 3d of Property.

The Second-Look Doctrine. Examples 14.9 and 14.10 illustrate that, for purposes of the common-law Rule and the Uniform Rule, both of which are concerned with the "time of creation" of the contingent future interest, interests created by the exercise of nongeneral powers or general testamentary powers are generally treated as "created" when the power was created. It is also true that the facts existing when the power was *exercised* can be taken into account. Taking this "second look" at the facts is a well-established procedure. The *second-look doctrine* is illustrated in the following example.

Example 14.13: Same disposition and appointment as in Example 14.10. At *G*'s death, *A* had two children, *X* and *Y*, but, unlike Example 14.10, *A* had no additional children after *G*'s death, and at *A*'s death *X* and *Y* were still living.

As in Example 14.10, the remainder in *A*'s grandchildren is considered to be created at *G*'s death. If only the facts existing at that point could be taken into account, the remainder interest would be invalid under the common-law Rule and would be allowed 90 years after *G*'s death to vest under the Uniform Rule. Under the second-look doctrine, however, the facts existing at A's death can be taken into account. Taking these facts into account saves A's appointment. At A's death, it has become clear that no additional children were born to A after G's death. Thus A's last surviving child will be either X or Y, both of whom were "in being" at G's death and therefore constitute the validating lives.

Note that if, after A's death, a third child (Z) was born to A, this would make the remainder in A's grandchildren invalid if Z survived A (this was the situation in Example 14.10). If Z predeceased A, however, the grandchildren's remainder would be validated by the second-look doctrine.

The second-look doctrine is a departure from the fundamental principle under the common-law Rule Against Perpetuities that only the facts existing when the contingent property interest was *created* can be taken into account in determining validity (see § 5.7 above). A persuasive justification put forward for this departure is that until the appointment is made the appointed interests cannot be known and their validity cannot be litigated. Thus no useful purpose would be served by holding appointed interests to be invalid because of what might have happened after the power was created but which at the time of exercise can no longer happen.

Another way of understanding and perhaps justifying the second-look doctrine is this. Restricting consideration to the facts existing when the power was created is out of the question. One post-creation fact that must be considered is the nature of the powerholder's appointment itself. If this fact could not be considered, no appointment, regardless of its terms, could ever be valid under the common-law Rule because of the *possibility* of the powerholder making an invalid appointment. Thus the nature of the actual appointment must be considered even though it is an event that occurred after the power was created. Although this amounts to taking a second look to determine the terms of the appointment, the process is rarely so described. Rather, if it is discussed at all, it is viewed as part of the fiction that the appointment "relates back" to the date of the power's creation. Some may therefore find it attractive to think of the second-look doctrine as nothing more than viewing the facts existing when the power was exercised as relating back along with the terms of the appointment.

A few cases and authorities have extended the second-look doctrine to gifts-in-default. See *Sears v. Coolidge*, 329 Mass. 340, 108 N.E.2d 563 (1952); *In re Frank*, 40 Pa. 116, 389 A.2d 536 (1978); Am. L. Prop. § 24.36; but see Simes & Smith on Future Interests § 1276.   Under this approach, the gift-in-default clause is judged on the facts existing at the time of *non*-exercise. Consider the following example.

Example 14.14: A was the life income beneficiary of a trust and the powerholder of a nongeneral power over the succeeding remainder interest. In default of appointment, the income after *A*'s death was to be paid to his children for the life of the survivor, and on the death of *A*'s last surviving child, the corpus was to be paid to *A*'s then-living grandchildren. *A*'s mother, *G*, who predeceased him, created the trust in her will. At *G*'s death, *A* had two children, *X* and *Y*. *A* died without having additional children and without exercising the power. *A* was survived by *X* and *Y*.

The gift-in-default was created at *G*'s death. Nevertheless, a second look at the facts existing at *A*'s death validates the gift-in-default under both the common-law Rule and the Uniform Rule. The validating lives are *X* and *Y*. Without a second look, the remainder interest in A's grandchildren would be invalid under the common-law Rule and subject to the 90-year permissible vesting period under the Uniform Rule. When G died, there was a possibility that A might have an additional child later, that such after-born child might survive A, and that such child might have a child (a grandchild of A) more than 21 years after the death of the survivor of A, X, and Y.

The second-look doctrine is not relevant to the perpetuity analysis under the Rule as reformulated in the Restatement 3d of Property, because that Rule does not depend on identifying the time of an interest's creation. Rather, the Rule depends on identifying the "transferor." The trust or other donative disposition of property must terminate on or before the end of the generations-based perpetuity period—in other words, on or before the death of the last surviving beneficiary of the disposition no more than two generations younger than the transferor.

§ 14.5 Appointed Powers

The powerholder of a power of appointment might exercise it by creating another power of appointment. The validity of the appointed power and the validity of its exercise are governed by the principles set forth in the preceding sections. Consider the following example.

Example 14.15: G devised land to his daughter A for life, remainder to such of A's descendants as A shall appoint. At her death, A exercised her nongeneral power by appointing to her son M (G's grandson) for life, remainder to such of M's descendants as M shall appoint. At his death, M exercised his nongeneral power by appointing to his son X (G's great-grandson) for life, remainder to X's then-living children.

A and M were living at G's death. X was born after G's death. A died after X was born, survived by M and X. M then died survived by X.

Analysis of M's power under the common-law Rule and the Uniform Rule. M's power is valid under the common-law Rule and under the Uniform Rule. M is the validating life because M was alive at G's death and cannot exercise his nongeneral power beyond his own death. If M had been born after G's death, however, M's power would have been invalid under the common-law Rule and would have been given 90 years after G's death to be exercised under the Uniform Rule.

Analysis of the exercise of M's power under the common-law Rule and the Uniform Rule. Although *M*'s power is valid, his exercise is partly invalid under the common-law Rule. The remainder in *X*'s children violates the Rule because it is a class gift subject to increase beyond a life in being at *G*'s death plus 21 years. Since *M*'s power was a nongeneral power, *M*'s appointment relates back and is treated as having been made by *A*. If *M*'s appointment related back no farther than that, of course, it would have been valid because *X* was alive at *A*'s death. However, *A*'s power was also a nongeneral power, so *M*'s appointment relates back another step. Because *M*'s appointment is now absorbed into *A*'s appointment, it is treated as having been made by *G*. Since *X* was not alive at *G*'s death, *X* cannot be the validating life. And, since *X* might have children more than 21 years after the deaths of *A* and *M* and any other person who was "in being" at *G*'s death, the remainder in *X*'s children is invalid at common law.

Under the Uniform Rule, the remainder in *X*'s children is not initially invalid. Instead, it is valid if *X* dies within 90 years after *G*'s death.

Analysis of M's power and its exercise under the Rule as reformulated in the Restatement 3d of Property. M's power is valid under the Rule as reformulated in the Restatement 3d of Property. When a nongeneral power creates a nongeneral power, the relation-back doctrine is applied twice. G is therefore considered to be the transferor of the disposition creating M's power. The power will terminate at M's death. This is within the generations-based perpetuity period, so the power is valid.

The exercise of M's power also is valid. The disposition created by the exercise of M's power (a life estate in X, followed by a remainder in X's children) is a trust for the "sole current benefit of a named individual who is more than two generations younger than the transferor...." Restatement 3d of Property § 27.1(b)(2). (See the excerpt in § 5.16 above.) In such a circumstance, the named individual—X—is a measuring life.

Note that if the disposition created by the exercise of M's power was a trust for the benefit of more than one current beneficiary, then X would not count as a measuring life (because X is three generations below the transferor, G). In that event, the disposition

would be subject to judicial modification under
Restatement 3d of Property § 27.2.

EXERCISES ON PART IV

1. Identify the parties to, and classify, the following powers of appointment:

a. *G* transferred land "to *A* for life, remainder to such persons as *D* shall appoint, otherwise to *T*."

b. *G* transferred land "to *A* for life, remainder to such charities as *D* shall appoint, otherwise to *T*."

c. *G* transferred land "to *A* for life, remainder to such charities as *A* shall by will appoint, otherwise to *T*."

d. *G* transferred property in trust, "to pay the income to *A* for life, then to distribute the corpus to X Charity. However, *A* may at any time direct the trustee to pay the trust corpus outright to *B*."

2. *G* conveyed property into a revocable trust providing for the payment of income to *A* for life, then for outright distribution of the corpus to such persons as *X* may appoint, otherwise to *B*. *G* died with substantial debts. *X* died without exercising the power, but with substantial debts and a surviving spouse, *S*. What result?

ANSWERS TO EXERCISES

Part I

1.a. Under the traditional system of classification, *A* has a life estate *pur autre vie* and *G* has an indefeasibly vested reversion. Under the simplified system in the Restatement 3d of Property, *A* has a life estate for the life of another and *G* has a vested reversion.

b. Under the traditional system of classification, *A* has a term of years and *B* has an indefeasibly vested remainder. Under the simplified system in the Restatement 3d of Property, *A* has a term of years and *B* has a vested reversion.

c. Under the traditional system of classification, *A* has a term of years, *B* has a contingent remainder, and *G* has a reversion that is vested subject to divestment. Under the simplified system in the Restatement 3d of Property, *A* has a term of years, *B* has a contingent remainder, and *G* has a contingent reversion.

d. Under the traditional system of classification, *A* has a life estate, *B* and *C* have alternative

361

contingent remainders, and *G* has a technical reversion that is vested subject to divestment. Under the simplified system in the Restatement 3d of Property, *A* has a life estate and *B* and *C* have contingent remainders.

e. Under the traditional system of classification, *A* has a life estate, *B* and *C* have contingent remainders, and *G* has a reversion that is vested subject to divestment. Under the simplified system in the Restatement 3d of Property, *A* has a life estate, *B* and *C* have contingent remainders, and *G* has a contingent reversion.

f. Under the traditional system of classification, *A* has a life estate, *B* has a remainder that is vested subject to divestment, and *C* has a shifting executory interest, which is contingent (based on the condition precedent that *B* not survive *A*). Under the simplified system in the Restatement 3d of Property, *A* has a life estate, and *B* and *C* have contingent remainders. If B dies before *A*, *C*'s interest becomes remainder that is indefeasibly vested (in the traditional system) and vested (under the Restatement 3d of Property).

g. Under the traditional system of classification, *A* has a fee simple determinable, and *B* has an executory interest that is contingent. Under the simplified system in the Restatement 3d of Property, *A* has a fee simple defeasible, and *B* has a contingent remainder. Note that in either case, *B*'s interest is invalid under the common-law Rule Against Perpetuities and may become invalid (and subject to judicial modification) under the Uniform Rule and the Rule as reformulated in the Restatement 3d of Property.

2.a. *D* has a remainder that is vested subject to open. The unborn or unadopted children of *A* have executory interests contingent on being born or adopted and on reaching age 30. The class is open at *G*'s death to future children—in other words, the rule of convenience does not then apply—because the time of distribution is *A*'s death, not *G*'s death. The validity of the class gift is governed by the all-or-nothing rule. The executory interests are invalid, so the entire class gift is invalid.

b. The interest in the first child of *A* to reach age 30 is a contingent remainder. In a jurisdiction without the rule of the destructibility of contingent remainders, the interest is invalid under the Rule Against Perpetuities, because there is no validating life. (*D* might not be the first child to reach age 30.) In a jurisdiction with the destructibility rule, however, the interest is valid: the contingent remainder will either vest in possession or be destroyed at A's death, so A is the validating life.

c. Before evaluating the effect of the Rule, one must classify the interests. G has created a term of years in A, followed by a remainder in G's "heirs at law." This remainder triggers the doctrine of worthier title in the jurisdictions still recognizing the doctrine. In such jurisdictions, the remainder in G's heirs becomes a reversion in G. Reversions are always vested, hence not subject to the Rule Against Perpetuities. In a jurisdiction not recognizing the doctrine of worthier title, the remainder in G's heirs is valid under the Rule Against Perpetuities, because the heirs will be determined at G's death.

d. The remainder in B is indefeasibly vested, hence not subject to the Rule Against Perpetuities. The remainder for life in A's children who reach 30, however, is invalid. Being invalid, it is struck out. This accelerates B's remainder: the transfer reads in effect "to A for life, remainder to B." B's remainder thus vests in possession at A's death.

3. We need to "wait and see" whether the trust actually terminates on or before the expiration of

the generations-based perpetuity period in Restatement 3d of Property § 27.1(a). If the trust does not terminate on or before the expiration of that period, the trust is subject to judicial modification under § 27.2. The court should modify the trust by requiring it to terminate at the end of the perpetuity period, at which time the trust corpus should be distributed by representation to *G*'s then-living descendants.

Parts II and III

1.a. *X*, *B*, and *C* hold as tenants in common.

b. *H*, *B*, and *C* hold as tenants in common.

c. The land passes through *A*'s probate estate and is subject to *S*'s elective share (or right to dower, in the few states that preserve dower). The remaining portion passes to X Charity. All recipients hold as tenants in common.

2.a. The transfer severs the tenancy (and the right of survivorship) between *A* and *B* and between *A* and *C*. *X* holds as tenant in common with *B* and with *C*. *B* and *C* hold as joint tenants (with the right of survivorship) with each other.

b. The right of survivorship operates at *A*'s death. *H* receives nothing.

c. Property held by the decedent and one or more third parties in joint tenancy is traditionally not subject to the surviving spouse's elective share or dower. In such a jurisdiction, the land would pass automatically to *B* and *C*, with nothing for *S* or X Charity. The Uniform Probate Code, however, entitles *S* to an elective share in the joint-tenancy property.

3. *G* has used the language of concurrent estates incorrectly. Joint tenancies have a right of survivorship; tenancies in common do not. A court will have to interpret the language to determine which tenancy *G* intended to create. In so doing, the court may use a canon of construction. This fact-pattern is drawn from *Camp v. Camp*, 220 Va. 595, S.E.2d 243 (1979). Relying on the canon that where two clauses are inconsistent the first one governs, the court in *Camp* held that the parties received the land as tenants in common. Whether this result accords with *G*'s most probable intention is a question you should ponder.

Part IV

1.a. *G* is the donor. *D* is the powerholder. The permissible appointees are any one or more persons. *T* is the taker in default. The power is presently exercisable, general, and collateral.

b. *G* is the donor. *D* is the powerholder. The permissible appointees are any one or more charities. *T* is the taker in default. The power is presently exercisable, nongeneral, and collateral.

c. *G* is the donor. *A* is the powerholder. The permissible appointees are any one or more charities. *T* is the taker in default. The power is testamentary, nongeneral, and in gross.

d. *G* is the donor. *A* is the powerholder. The only permissible appointee is *B*. The taker in default is X Charity. The power is presently exercisable and nongeneral. With respect to the remainder interest, the power is in gross. With respect to *A*'s income interest, the power is appendant.

2. *G*'s creditors: under modern law, they are entitled to reach the trust assets, because a reserved power to revoke is the same as a reserved general power of appointment. *D*'s creditors: the majority view is that they are not able to reach the property, because *D* did not exercise the power. *D*'s surviving spouse: the traditional view is that the elective share is limited to the decedent's probate estate, which excludes property subject to a presently exercisable general power of appointment; the Uniform Probate Code reaches the opposite result in § 2-205(1)(i).

INDEX

References are to Pages

PERPETUITIES, RULE AGAINST
See Rule Against Perpetuities

PERSONALTY, INTERESTS IN
Estate planning, 8-10
Future interests in favor of grantor's heirs, subject to
      Worthier Title Doctrine, see Worthier Title
      Doctrine
Remainders in,
      Indestructible, see Destructibility Rule
      Unaffected by Rule in Shelley's Case, see Rule in
      Shelley's Case

POSSESSORY ESTATES
    See Estate at Sufference; Estate at Will; Estate from
      Period to Period; Fee Simple Absolute; Fee
      Simple Determinable; Fee Simple Subject to a
      Condition Subsequent; Fee Simple Subject to an
      Executory Limitation; Fee Tail; Life Estates;
      Terms of Years

POSSIBILITIES OF REVERTER
    See also Contingent Interests; Reversionary Interests;
      Worthier Title Doctrine
Alienability of, see Alienability
Ambiguous language, construction problems, 55-58
Defined, 45
Enforcement of, 48-49
Indestructible, see Destructibility Rule
Restatement 3d of Property, 62
Rule Against Perpetuities, see Rule Against Perpetuities
Rule in Shelley's Case, see Rule in Shelley's Case

ABOUT THE AUTHORS

Thomas P. Gallanis is the N. William Hines Chair in Law at the University of Iowa. He is the Executive Director of the Joint Editorial Board for Uniform Trust and Estate Acts and an Adviser to the ALI project on the Principles of the Law of Nonprofit Organizations. He was Associate Reporter for the Restatement Third of Trusts and participated in the Members Consultative Group for the Restatement Third of Property: Wills and Other Donative Transfers. He also served as the Reporter for the Uniform Real Property Transfer on Death Act, codified as part of the Uniform Probate Code, and the Uniform Powers of Appointment Act.

Lawrence W. Waggoner is the Lewis M. Simes Professor Emeritus of Law at the University of Michigan. He was the Reporter for the Restatement Third of Property: Wills and Other Donative Transfers and the Director of Research of the Joint Editorial Board for Uniform Trust and Estate Acts. He was the principal architect and draftsperson of the 1990 and 2008 revisions of the Uniform Probate Code. He served as Reporter for several other uniform acts, including the Uniform Statutory Rule Against Perpetuities. He was also an Adviser to the Restatement Third of Trusts.